D1491316

Sex Roles in the State House

Sex Roles
in the
State House

IRENE DIAMOND

NEW HAVEN AND LONDON,
YALE UNIVERSITY PRESS,
1977

Published with assistance from the
foundation established in memory of
Oliver Baty Cunningham of the Class
of 1917, Yale College.

Designed by Sally Sullivan
and set in Primer type.
Printed in the United States of America by
Vail-Ballou Press, Inc., Binghamton, N.Y.

Published in Great Britain, Europe, Africa, and
Asia by Yale University Press, Ltd., London.
Distributed in Latin America by Kaiman & Polon,
Inc., New York City; in Australia and New
Zealand by Book & Film Services, Artarmon,
N.S.W., Australia; and in Japan by Harper & Row,
Publishers, Tokyo Office.

Library of Congress Cataloging in Publication Data

Diamond, Irene, 1947–
    Sex roles in the state house.

    Includes index.
    1. Women in politics—New England.   2. Legislators—
New England.   3. Sex role.   I. Title.
HQ1391.U5D52   301.41′2′0974   76-49708
ISBN 0-300-02115-1

To the Memory of Richard R. Warner

Contents

Tables and Figures

ix

Figures

Preface

*And perhaps the sexes are more related than we think, and
the great renewal of the world will perhaps consist in this,
that man and maid, freed from all false feeling and aversion
will seek each other not as opposites, but as brother and sis-
ter, as neighbors, and will come together as human beings.*

Rilke, *Letters To a Young Poet*

What are the differences between the sexes? Are these differences changing? If so, what are the historical conditions
bringing about such changes? And most importantly, what is
the ultimate direction of these changes? What kind of society
will result? These are important questions, but not ones I could
presume to answer in the following pages; still I pose them here
because they are my most general concerns, and they do explain why I treat the subject of women in politics as I do.

The major hypothesis that I will develop and test—that sex
differentiation decreases as competition for political office increases—relates to the sexes and politics in contemporary America. State legislatures are the particular focus because this is the
one political arena where the question of sex differences can be
examined in a systematic and quantitative fashion. Chapter 1
develops the model of sex differentiation and politics, while the
remaining chapters explore its usefulness. Chapters 2 and 3 out-
line the broad contours of sex differences in state legislative politics, while chapters 4 and 5 examine in some depth interpersonal relationships and psychological orientations. On the basis
of my findings on women in state legislatures, I will consider,
in the final chapter, what might be necessary in order to create
a polity where politics is not the domain of one sex.

My investigation is perhaps a bit unusual in that it employs
several data-gathering techniques. I imagine that some readers

will find certain of the techniques less satisfying for tackling the problem than others, but if I convince the skeptical reader of the worth of at least one, I will be satisfied.

In chapter 2 I make use of aggregate data that enable me to identify the structural factors explaining why women are more readily elected to the legislature in certain areas than in others. In chapter 3 I turn to survey data in order to explore both the behavioral differences between female and male legislators and the conditions that modify these differences. Chapters 4 and 5 flesh out through personal interviews many of the findings and propositions of the previous chapters. In order to give the reader a more intimate understanding of the problems that women in politics face, I have preserved, as much as I could, the verbatim accounts of several women legislators. These latter chapters will be of particular interest to the reader who desires a more intimate understanding of the specific problems and life circumstances of women in politics.

I could not have completed this project without the support and criticism of others. It is customary when acknowledging such help to thank each person for her/his particular contribution and to do so in a ritualized order which effectively establishes a hierarchy of importance among endeavors. In working toward that society where the sexes will come together as complete human beings I would like to simply thank each of the wonderful people who have helped me along the way. Thank you! Marian Neal Ash, Florence Berry, Maureen Bushkovitch, Greg Caldeira, Roberta Cohen, Glenn Diamond, Myra Marx Ferree, Estelle Freedman, Robert Hammel, Michael Kagy, Duane Lockard, Ruth Mandel, Edward R. Tufte, Alan Wertheimer, and Ellen Woodbury.

In keeping with an element of the tradition that is worthy of retention I will note that I alone am responsible for all the weaknesses in this work.

The book was completed while I was a Visiting Research Associate at the Center for the American Woman and Politics, Eagleton Institute of Politics, Rutgers University.

1: Sex, Competition, and Politics

In some parts of New Guinea . . . women grow sweet potatoes and men grow yams, and yams are the prestige food, the food one distributes at feasts.

Michelle Zimbalist Rosaldo

Occupations are universally sex-typed; most are held predominantly or exclusively by one sex or the other. What is "female" and what is "male" may differ somewhat from society to society, but prestige values always attach to male activities.[1] Politics is preeminently male. Why this is so is a question virtually ignored in the twentieth century until the emergence of the contemporary women's movement in the late 1960s. One can speculate as to why women have not been as involved in politics as men, but unfortunately it is very difficult to study something that has not occurred. We cannot find places where women have shared power equally with men and then make comparisons with places where power has not been shared. American state legislatures do, however, provide a useful focus for tackling this question.

State legislators are predominantly male, but interestingly there is some variation from state to state in the degree of male domination. In 1971 Alabama, for example, had one female legislator, while New Hampshire had seventy-one. Why are women more frequently elected in certain states than in others? The model put forth here, developed in response to this question, may also prove relevant to the more general concern of women and politics. Other more specific questions flow from the initial problem of state-to-state differences. Are different types of women elected where the legislature is less exclusively

1

male? Do female legislators behave differently from male legislators? And finally, what happens to the institution and to these
women when this male bastion is breached?

In areas where norms and attitudes about sex roles are in
flux—where traditional notions about appropriate sex-role behavior are declining and more modern notions stressing change
and flexibility are emerging—women might be expected to experience less difficulty in entering a traditionally male occupation. Sex-role specialization generally erodes more quickly in
urban areas. Data on voting participation and interest in politics—both in the United States and elsewhere—show conclu-
sively that sex differences are less sharp in urban areas than in
rural areas.[2] Do these urban-rural differences hold when politics
becomes an occupation? Here it is more difficult to generalize
because the number of instances in which politics has become
an occupation for women is very limited. In Scandinavia women
are elected in significantly larger numbers in urban areas than
in rural areas, on both the local and national levels.[3] Within the
United States, among those few women who have been elected
to the House of Representatives on their own (not appointed or
specially elected to fill vacancies), a disproportionate number
have come from urban states.[4] On this basis urban states should
have a higher proportion of women legislators than rural states.
But, contrary to expectation, the relatively rural states of New
England have been in the vanguard.

There are two possible explanations for this phenomenon. Either some other factor is overriding the presumed effects of urbanization, or else the legislative job is not even comparable in
urban and rural states. If a legislative seat is viewed as an important step in one state's ladder of political advancement, then
the expectations for a state legislator might differ considerably
from those in a state where a legislative seat amounts to a political dead end. (In the latter case it is likely that the position of
state legislator is not even viewed as a credible occupation.) Political dead ends are generally low-status positions (with the no-
table exception of the presidency) and therefore do not stimu-

late intense competition. Low-status positions are not likely to attract the politically ambitious, and men are more typically ambitious than females. Outside politics there is clearly an inverse relationship between the desirability of an occupation—the prestige and rewards associated with it—and the proportion of women in the occupation.[5] The situation of doctors compared to that of nurses in American society is only one of innumerable examples one could cite. These patterns suggest that women should be more common in legislatures where the seat is not a status position—or, alternatively, where competition for access to the seat is not very intense. Political competition conceived of as a function of the desirability of the office reduces the two possible explanations to one: political competition may override the effects of urbanization, and at the same time change the nature of the legislative job. On this basis we can predict that the sex composition of legislatures is inversely related to competition for legislative seats. Where competition for seats is intense few women will hold seats and where competition is less intense larger numbers of women will hold seats: as competition declines the proportion of women will rise.

We know that the nature of the legislative job is in fact different from state to state. Legislatures differ in what is expected of the typical legislator. They vary in their degree of professionalism—that is, the extent to which the legislator pursues political work as an avocation and not simply as a vocation. The polar types are the citizen legislature and the professional legislature. In the citizen legislature the typical member is an individual with little political experience and no long-term commitment to politics as a career: politics is an avocation and a seat in the legislature is simply an opportunity for pursuing volunteer work. In the professional legislature the typical member has prior political experience and holds a long-term commitment to politics as a vocation: a seat in the legislature is one step in a lifelong political career. The typical occupation of this legislator, as with the majority of serious politicians in this country, is the legal profession. Political scientists often measure professionalism by looking at such indicators as the extent of the legislators' prior political experience, the rate of turnover, and the percentage of lawyers.[6] The use of such measurements implies that professionalism is a simple continuum, particular legislatures being either low or high in certain characteristics. If, however, the concern is with the requirements of the legislative role—the recruitment process the individual is expected to follow, the values the individual is expected to hold, and so forth—professionalism might be usefully visualized as a cone representing increasing restrictiveness of role requirements from the least to the most professional legislature. The base of the cone represents the citizen legislature, whose requirements are very loose and unrestrictive: the resources needed by the legislator—who might be a bartender or an automobile dealer—are unspecified. (A vivid example of nonprofessionalism is New Hampshire's large citizen legislature, a member of which, after being convicted of stealing an ambulance and committed to a local mental institution, was subsequently reelected and allowed, as part of his course of therapy, to fulfill his legislative duties and return to the mental institution each evening.) The peak of the cone represents the professional legislature, with fairly rigorous and restrictive requirements: the resources needed by the legislator are very specific, so that the legislator cannot be the average citizen with a passing interest in politics.

How does this relate to the recruitment and election of female legislators? The model predicts that women are more likely to obtain seats when the competition for office is minimal, a situation often associated with a nonselective recruitment process. In other words, the noncompetitive situation is likely to be the nonprofessional situation. When the demand for the product is low, the seller cannot be choosy about prospective buyers. The political recruiter in a low-demand situation cannot ask that potential candidates possess specific qualifications; the politically inexperienced—even women—become acceptable. Moreover, women in low-demand situations become acceptable to themselves as prospective candidates. They can become motivated because the situation offers them a possibility of success that can be achieved with minimal cost; that is, basic life patterns do not have to be substantially altered.

The dynamic is entirely different where political competition is stiff. In this high-demand—and typically professional—situation, the political recruiter can select prospective candidates by eliminating those contestants who do not meet a set of specific criteria: sex, occupational background, and political experience become relevant.[7] The selective standards established by the recruitment process are in turn reinforced by the voters' own selection procedures, because voters' expectations of a proper candidate are largely a function of what they have been offered previously. (Catholicism was no longer much of an issue in selecting presidential candidates after the election of John F. Kennedy). The self-selection process in the competitive situation should operate to reduce the pool of motivated women, not only because of women's realistic assessment of their opportunities, but also because the pool of women with the requisite resources is small. One consequence of traditional sex-role practices is that there are few women who have the skills, experience, or time demanded by the more competitive situation. For women who hold the traditional values, success here can be achieved only at considerable cost (disruption of family life, and so forth), and few women are willing to incur these costs. (The perception of costs is related to different role orientations and this is the subject of chapter 5).

Since competitive professional recruitment structures are necessarily selective and demanding, it follows that individuals who do not meet one of the criteria for acceptability need to compensate for such deficiencies by meeting the remaining ones. Therefore, if a woman—who by definition lacks the proper sex criterion—survives a competitive elimination process, it is likely that she has the other requisite criteria. The woman legislator elected in a competitive situation will probably have a career pattern similar to that of her male counterpart, and such a similarity should have consequences for legislative behavior. It has been shown that preincumbency roles are important in ex-

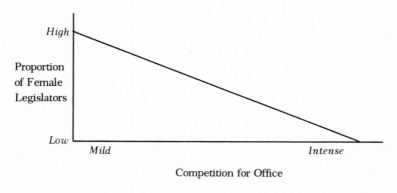

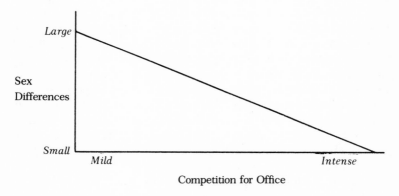

Figure 1.1   Sex and Competition for Office

plaining the behavior of incumbents.[8] Therefore, if a woman
legislator's experience prior to her election includes a male career pattern, her behavior in the legislature should bear a
greater resemblance to that of the average male legislator than
to that of the woman legislator whose prior experience included
only traditional feminine roles. The preincumbency roles demanded by a selective recruitment process should serve to
lessen or counteract the effects of traditional sex-role socialization. The model can now account for behavioral differences as

well: political competition is inversely related to both the proportion of female legislators and the degree of sex-related differences in legislatures. The probability that a woman will be elected to the legislature under conditions of intense political competition is low; however, the probability that a woman who is elected under such conditions will resemble a man in her career pattern and legislative behavior is high.

This model has been developed within the context of a discussion of state legislatures, but it is applicable to legislative bodies at other levels and can explain the patterns across levels of legislative bodies. The effects of competition will be most evident at the most competitive, that is, the national level. A vivid example is seen in the 1972 congressional election. All five of the new congresswomen elected in November 1972 were lawyers, and each had either held elective office at the county or state level or served as legal counsel for a statewide organization.[9] In a study of recruitment of women for Congress, Bullock and Heys noted distinct differences in recruitment patterns between regularly elected congresswomen and those who achieved their position through widow's succession—a distinctly nonselective process. During the period 1917–70, 20 percent of the regularly elected women were lawyers, whereas none of the widows was a lawyer; 69 percent of the regularly elected women, but only 10 percent of the widows, had held a public office before entering Congress. Also,

> 57% of the regularly elected women, but only 21% of all freshmen, listed party activities. These data suggest that political experience is more crucial for women than men who wish to be elected to Congress.[10]

This latter finding provides support for my hypothesis that a woman, who by definition lacks one of the requisite criteria for office, must compensate by fulfilling the others.

2: Female Legislators: Where Are They?

The traditional test of competition for office deals with competition between political parties and is commonly measured by using electoral data and data on turnover in office—in effect testing the party's ability to dominate offices within a state.[1] But such measures say nothing about the desirability of a particular office—about what status the position has. It is this aspect of competition that is most crucial when considering the recruitment of women.

The status or desirability of a legislative seat or any political office is a complex function, deriving from both individual needs and societal norms. Four measurable factors are considered here:

1. perceived difficulty of obtaining the office—how selective the recruitment process is
2. perceived rewards of the office
3. perceived powers of the office
4. number of other officeholders holding the same powers

When opportunities to obtain a legislative seat are limited, competition is likely to be intense and therefore the number of women who obtain seats small. Women have a greater chance of obtaining seats when opportunities are more extensive—when there are more seats to go around. Legislatures vary in size from state to state, but state populations vary too. Hence the chance of obtaining a seat is not a function of legislative size alone but of size adjusted for state population. A two-part hypothesis is now possible:

First: the percentage of the legislature that consists of women will vary directly with the number of seats per 100,000 persons.

A high seats-to-population ratio means greater potential opportunities and hence less competiton, while a low seats-to-population ratio means fewer opportunities and hence more competition.

Second: since competition is also likely to be more intense when the rewards are greater—when the office is more lucrative—the percentage of the legislature that consists of women will vary inversely with legislative salaries.

Examination of the data across states for the 1971 legislative session indicates that it is almost meaningless to talk about the proportion of women state senators. The absolute number of women in individual state senates varies from zero to four: 23 chambers have no women, 17 have one, 6 have two, 2 have three, and 2 have four (appendix 2). The proportions—which vary from 0 percent to 13 percent because of the greater variation in the absolute sizes of senates—are based on very small absolute differences. Upper houses are considerably smaller than lower houses and so in *all* states the number of senate positions is limited. There is no observable correlation between senate seats per 100,000 population and the proportion of women senators. Upper houses are just that—"upper." The perceived powers are greater, and, since fewer persons share those powers, any individual in the body has a greater chance of obtaining a leadership position. All of this spells status and no women. The representation of women in the upper houses of state legislatures is comparable to the sparse representation of women in the United States Senate. Only ten women have ever served in the Senate, and all ten were first elected or appointed to Congress to fill the unexpired terms of men (their husbands in most cases) who had resigned or died in office. Only three women have been elected to full six-year terms.[2] This is a marked contrast to the situation in state senates, whose recruitment patterns (1955 to 1973) indicate that the female senator need not be a widow carrying on for her husband.

Though female representation in state senates is not explained by competition for senate seats, the scatterplot in figure

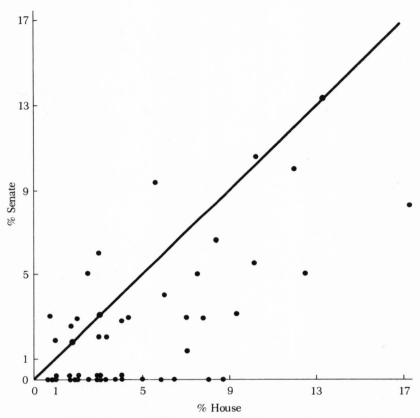

Figure 2.1   Percentage of Women in Senate, by Percentage of Women in House

2.1 indicates a systematic pattern. Women are less likely to be elected to the upper houses: the average proportion in the senates is 2.5 percent, whereas the average proportion in the lower houses is 4.9 percent. Twenty-three states have no women in their senates, but most of these states also have a small proportion of women in their lower houses. The only states with a relatively high proportion of women in the upper houses are states which have an even higher proportion in their lower houses. "Modest representation" of women in the upper house is dependent on their "substantial representation" in the lower house. More specifically, the average proportion in the upper house is approximately 60 percent of the proportion in the lower house.[3] The sheer fact of the senate's being "upper" partially explains the sparse representation of women, but the extent to which women are represented in upper houses is also related to their lower house representation. Lack of an established tradition is one explanation for women's low level of political officeholding, but where such a tradition exists it is easier for women to enter the political arena. Several of the women legislators interviewed in New Hampshire made comments such as, "No, it was not difficult for me because there were women before in my district." If barriers are broken in the lower house, there is a greater likelihood that they will be broken in the upper house— even though the favorable conditions do not obtain. Party recruiters and voters are more likely to be receptive to a female candidacy for the senate if they have grown accustomed to women in the lower house. Also, because recruitment for the upper house is more selective, previous legislative service per se may increase the likelihood of a successful candidacy. Where more women have served in the lower house, there is simply a greater pool of potential candidates "available" for election to the upper. Of the 43 women serving in state senates in 1971, 26 previously served in lower houses. But beyond these factors, the relationship between senate and house representation is also accounted for by the likelihood that the status and hence actual competition for senate seats is affected by the status of lower house seats.

In lower houses there is considerable variation in the representation of women. In 1971 the New Hampshire house had 68 women, constituting 17 percent of that oversized body. Texas, on the other hand, had only 1 woman out of a total of 150 lower house representatives. The proportion of women representatives is related to the basic measure of competition for office: seats per 100,000 persons explains 21 percent of the variation in the proportion of women.[4] The ability of women to obtain legislative seats is related to the number of opportunities for obtaining seats: as opportunities relative to the population of a state increase, the proportion of women in the legislature increases. It is important to note that it is the size of the legislture *relative to the population* which is the significant explanatory variable. The size of the house itself bears little relationship to the representation of women; in fact, if deviant New Hampshire is excluded from the calculations, size is inversely related to the proportion of women. When New Hampshire is included there appears to be a slight positive relationship between size and the proportion of women ($r = .10$). But when New Hampshire is excluded it turns out that the relationship is a negative one ($r = -.36$): in other words, the larger houses actually tend to have lower proportions of women. Close examination of figure 2.2 indicates why the correlation is negative when New Hampshire is excluded.

The New Hampshire legislature has 400 members. The next largest legislature is that of Massachusetts, with 240. This difference means that New Hampshire in effect occupies the entire right segment of the graph. The rest of the states, which are situated in the left segment, show a negative relationship between size and the proportion of women. New Hampshire, isolated in the upper right portion, distorts this relationship. The graph indicates then that the correlation based on the exclusion of New Hampshire allows for a more accurate summary of the relationship between size and proportion of women. Figure 2.2 further indicates that the only states with large legislatures and a high proportion of women are four New England states—Connecticut, Maine, New Hampshire, and Vermont, the four least densely populated states in New England. The emphasis on town autonomy peculiar to New England, which prior to reapportionment generally allotted each town a representative in the state legislature, has resulted in large legislative bodies relative to population.[5] And it appears that a by-product of this emphasis has been heavier representation of women in comparison to other regions. Outside New England large legislatures are invariably associated with large populations.[6] The correlation between house size and population, excluding oversized New Hampshire, is .52. Generally the more populated states have

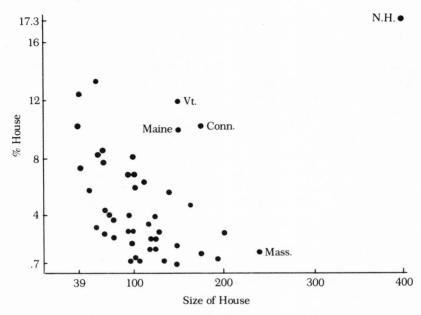

Figure 2.2   Percentage of Women in House, by Size of House

large legislatures: but since increases in legislative size do not keep pace with increases in population, competition for legislative seats generally increases in the more heavily populated states (r = − .61), and here the proportion of women legislators is lower (r = − .46). The size of the legislature relative to the population—competition for seats—is the critical variable when explaining female representation in the lower houses of state legislatures: as competition for seats decreases the proportion of women legislators increases.

We also predicted, on the basis of the model, that there would be a relationship between the rewards of office and the sex composition of legislatures. There is a modest relationship between salary and the proportion of women, but the central question is whether salary has an *independent* effect. This does not seem to be the case. The effects of salary cannot be isolated from competition for seats. It is the latter that is the more powerful explanatory variable.[7] Moreover, the explanatory power of salary is largely a function of deviant New Hampshire. New Hampshire, in addition to having an oversized legislature, pays its legislators $200 biennially, a "wage" considerably lower than that of any other state (the average biennial legislative salary nationally is $13,107). If New Hampshire is excluded from the calculations, the relationship between salary and proportion of women falls apart. Salary then is not particularly useful in explaining the pattern *across* the states but, as will be demonstrated in later chapters, it is certainly a significant factor in explaining why New Hampshire has had more women legislators than any other state.

Analysis of Residuals

Since this is a largely exploratory project, "exposure, the effective laying open of the data to display the unanticipated," is particularly appropriate.[8] Examination of the table of residuals permits such exposure. Table 2.1 reports the actual proportions of women legislators and the predicted proportions—the predictions made by knowing a state's competition-for-seats ratio. The difference between an actual proportion and the predicted proportion is called the residual—that part of a state's proportion of female legislators which is unexplained by the state's seats ratio.

The South

Table 2.1 indicates that all but one of the southern states have fewer women in their legislatures than predicted by the equation (negative residuals). This underrepresentation of women in the southern states relative to other regions is not surprising in light of the history of the South. The ideological rhetoric of the plantation culture placed white women on a pedestal, isolating them from normal economic and social inter-

Table 2.1 Residual Analysis of Percentage of
Female Legislators in Lower House

South	Actual	Predicted	Residual
Georgia	1.0	4.6	−3.6
South Carolina	1.6	4.9	−3.3
Arkansas	2.0	5.1	−3.1
Alabama	1.0	3.9	−2.9
Mississippi	2.4	5.2	−2.8
Virginia	1.0	3.2	−2.2
Texas	.7	2.4	−1.7
North Carolina	1.7	3.4	−1.7
Louisiana	2.9	3.8	− .8
Florida	3.4	2.8	+ .5
New England			
New Hampshire	17.2	11.1	+6.1
Connecticut	10.2	5.4	+4.8
Rhode Island	3.0	6.8	−3.8
Massachusetts	1.7	4.6	−2.9
Vermont	12.0	9.9	+2.1
Maine	9.3	7.7	+1.6
West			
Arizona	13.3	4.1	+9.2
Montana	1.0	7.7	−6.8
Nevada	12.5	6.2	+6.3
Wyoming	3.3	8.2	−5.0
Oregon	8.3	3.8	+4.5
Washington	8.1	3.8	+4.3
Colorado	7.7	3.8	+3.0
Utah	8.7	5.6	+3.1
New Mexico	2.8	5.7	+2.9
California	3.8	1.0	+2.8
Idaho	4.3	6.6	+2.3
Alaska	7.5	7.4	+1.1
Hawaii	5.9	5.7	+ .2
Midwest			
Michigan	6.4	2.2	+4.2
Indiana	7.1	3.0	+4.1
North Dakota	4.1	7.9	−3.8
Minnesota	.7	4.2	−3.5
South Dakota	4.0	7.0	−3.0
Kansas	2.4	5.2	−2.8
Iowa	6.0	4.2	+1.8
Ohio	3.0	1.8	+1.2
Illinois	1.7	2.7	−1.0
Wisconsin	3.0	3.3	− .2

Table 2.1 (*Continued*)

Mid-Atlantic	Actual	Predicted	Residual
Delaware	10.2	5.8	+4.4
New Jersey	2.5	2.1	+ .4
New York	2.0	1.7	+ .3
Pennsylvania	3.0	2.8	+ .2
Border			
West Virginia	7.0	4.7	+2.3
Tennessee	2.0	3.5	−1.5
Oklahoma	3.0	4.4	−1.4
Maryland	5.6	4.3	+1.3
Missouri	4.9	4.2	+ .7
Kentucky	4.0	3.9	+ .1

Note: A negative residual indicates that a state had a lower percentage of female legislators than predicted on the basis of its competition-for-seats ratio. A positive residual indicates that it had a higher percentage than predicted.

course to a greater extent than women in other areas of the country.[9] This same pattern of underrepresentation appears on the national level as well: prior to the Ninety-third Congress seventeen women from southern states served in Congress, but only two were elected at regular elections.[10] Since 1921, when women first began serving in state legislatures, women legislators have been an anomaly in southern politics: the all-time high was 5 women in the Mississippi house in 1967, but 2 of the 5 gained their seats through widow's succession.

For 1971 Florida is the only southern state in which the predicted proportion of women is less than the actual proportion, and Florida had the highest rate of population change of any southern state during the 1950s and 1960s. Its population increased by 78.7 percent from 1950 to 1960 and by 37.1 percent from 1960 to 1970. This rapid growth was not a result of any dramatic change in Florida's birthrate but of considerable population movement into the state from other regions.[11] The massive influx of nonsoutherners has had a marked effect on Florida's voting patterns, moving it out of the safely Democratic column and in effect nationalizing its voting patterns.[12] Thus prevailing cultural attitudes toward women could be expected to undergo modification, with some eventual impact on the political participation of women.

This growing similarity between Florida and the rest of the nation is a product of the changes taking place in southern Florida. All five women serving in the 1971 session were elected from districts in the southern half of the state, where most of the population change has occurred. And except for the one black legislator none of these women were born in Florida.

New England

No other regional grouping displays any kind of systematic pattern, but the question of why Massachusetts and Rhode Island do not have the high proportions of women found in the rest of New England needs some examination. Massachusetts fits the New England pattern in that it has an oversized legislature (the second largest in the nation), but it has fewer women than predicted. Rhode Island's lower house, with 100 seats, is not particularly large in absolute size; but, since the population of the state is just under one million, its seats ratio falls within the New England pattern. Nevertheless, like Massachusetts, Rhode Island has fewer women legislators than predicted. Furthermore, over time neither state has ever had a substantial representation of women: for the years 1955–69, for example, Massachusetts averaged 2.3 percent, and Rhode Island averaged 3.0 percent. Rhode Island and Massachusetts are part of the southern New England tradition: they are extensively industrialized and have large ethnic minorities. Connecticut shares these characteristics, but here the proportion of women legislators is higher than predicted.[13] In fact, Connecticut has considerably more women legislators than predicted, and Connecticut has also had a substantial representation of women over time as compared to other states.

This persistent difference over time among the southern New England states needs to be explained. Connecticut is the only one of these states to have reduced the size of its assembly in recent years, and it did so in response to the Supreme Court ruling in *Baker* v. *Carr* (1962), which mandated that state legislatures be apportioned on the basis of one person, one vote. Prior to reapportionment the Connecticut assembly was a far cry from the Court's democratic ideal. Duane Lockard noted in 1958: "The one-tenth of the people who live in the smallest towns have half the representation in the House. . . . Nearly 90 percent of these towns are regularly to be found in the Republican column on election day." [14] And historically a large proportion of the women elected to the house of representatives have come from these small Republican towns. The dynamic that brings about the anomalous situation of women advancing politically in rural Republican districts will be treated in greater depth in chapter 4. But in terms of the theoretical framework developed so far, it is not at all surprising that women have succeeded in rural Republican districts. In Connecticut, prior to reapportionment, these overrepresented districts were extremely noncompetitive—the situation most favorable for the election of women. Reapportionment and the overall reduction in the size of the Connecticut house of representatives have reduced the total number of representatives coming from these small towns, and consequently the absolute number of women serving in each session has declined. [15] From 1953 to 1965 there was an average of 44 women in the house during each legislative session, whereas from 1967 to 1971 there was an average of 19 per session. However, the pre-reapportionment days established certain precedents regarding the recruitment of women which have been maintained in the more competitive period that followed, and the Connecticut legislature today has a higher proportion of women than is predicted by its competition-for-seats ratio.

Connecticut stands in marked contrast to Massachusetts and Rhode Island, where reapportionment did not drastically alter the seats ratio. The Supreme Court directive to correct malapportioned legislatures did not have a profound impact on Massachusetts because here districting did not particularly favor small rural districts. [16] Massachusetts has always been significantly more populous than any of the other New England states, and hence its ratio of seats to population has deviated considerably from the rest of New England. Thus at no time did the structural features favorable to the election of women exist in Massachusetts.

Rhode Island presents a more perplexing problem. Its seats ratio falls within the New England pattern, and prior to reapportionment districting did favor the small towns.[17] But Rhode Island is also the most urbanized state in New England and has a higher proportion of immigrants and their second- and third-generation progeny than any other state—conditions which led to the domination of state politics by the Democrats.[18] The three women serving in the Rhode Island house in 1971 were all Republicans from small towns (their mean population was 8,161). It appears then that in Rhode Island structural conditions that might otherwise be favorable to the election of women have been cancelled out by the domination of the Democratic party. In Rhode Island "the Democratic party early became the spokesman for the underdog and disenfranchised immigrants," and in its role as spokesman for the ethnic working class it probably reflected the traditional values which historically have made for rigid sex-role differentiation within this class.[19] Given the political conditions in Rhode Island we an speculate that these norms probably worked to exclude women from politics in two ways. First, in most cases women were not even considered for positions because the traditional ideology militated against such consideration. Second, the high seats ratio suggests that recruitment might have been a problem; but the Democratic party probably did not have a very large pool of women available. The Democratic pool is more limited simply because working-class women are less likely to have time to become involved in partisan politics or community affairs, and historically women who have been involved in community affairs have usually been Republicans. The economic and cultural conditions leading to the dominance of the Democratic party appear to provide a partial explanation of why Rhode Island has fewer women than predicted.

Though Massachusetts never possessed the favorable structural conditions found in Rhode Island, it did share with Rhode Island the cultural, economic, and political factors that have discouraged the recruitment of women. Like Rhode Island, Massachusetts has a sizable proportion of ethnic minorities and is heavily urban. Though there is no reason to believe that urbanization per se is unfavorable to women, heavy concentrations of ethnics in urban centers has led to the emergence of a strong Democratic party in both states, and the latter has not been a favorable condition for the recruitment of women.

Having considered why Rhode Island and Massachusetts are not part of the New England "vanguard," we have a better grasp of the dynamics that have engendered a more equitable representation in the rest of New England. Minimal competition for legislative seats is crucial and, except for Massachusetts, this phenomenon has existed at one time or another in sections of each state. But minimal competition needs to be combined with the dominance of the Republican party either statewide, as in Maine, Vermont, and New Hampshire, or in significant geographical subsections, as in Connecticut prior to reapportionment. This initial confluence of factors creates a set of norms regarding the election of women legislators which makes it probable that women will be elected even when the initial conditions have been modified. Connecticut now elects more women legislators than is to be expected on the basis of its current competition for seats, and today all four states elect significant proportions of Democratic women.

Arizona

The South and New England present the only two cases of significant regional configuration. But examination of certain individual states can yield interesting results. Arizona has the largest residual of any state: the predicted proportion of women legislators is 4.1 percent, but the actual proportion is 13.3 percent. Moreover, this relatively high figure is not the result of something peculiar to 1971, for the proportion has been high since 1953, averaging 11.6 percent for the years 1953–69. Prior to reapportionment the Arizona house was not well apportioned, which suggests that the overrepresentation of women might be, as in Connecticut, the result of a districting that initially created conditions favorable to the election of women legislators.[20] But, unlike the situation in New England, in the Southwest the underrepresentation of urban centers has worked to the disadvantage of Republicans, for in this region it is the overrepresented rural areas which have traditionally supported the Democratic party.[21] The large majority of the women elected to the legislature in Arizona have been Republican, as in Connecticut, but in contrast to the Connecticut situation most of the women have come from the underrepresented urban and suburban areas. This phenomenon of the urban Republican woman was first observable in the 1953 legislative session. Prior to 1953 very few women had ever served in the lower house, and most of the pre-1953 women were Democrats; in 1953, however, the number of women shot up to 10 from the previous session's 3.[22] It was also in 1953 that Barry Goldwater began representing Arizona in the U.S. Senate. The jump in the number of women legislators and the success of Goldwater in this "modified one-party Democratic state" may be purely coincidental, but their occurrence in the same year suggests the *possibility* that the two phenomena have a common source—namely the moralistic strain in Arizona's political culture.

Daniel Elazar has argued that political life in any state can best be understood in light of the state's political culture—"the particular pattern of orientation to political action in which each political system is imbedded." This orientation influences perceptions of what politics is and what can be expected from government, the kinds of people who become politically active, and the way the "art" of government is practiced. Elazar describes three major political subcultures in the U.S.—the moralistic, the individualistic, and the traditionalistic—and posits that each state's culture has evolved from the population movement of various religious and ethnic groups with their distinct sociocultural patterns. According to this classification Arizona is the only one-party or modified one-party Democratic state with a strong moralistic strain in its political culture.[23]

> In the moralistic political culture, both the general public and the politician conceive of politics as a public activity centered on some notion of the public good and properly devoted to the advancement of the public interest. Good government, then, is measured by the degree to which it promotes the public good and in terms of the *honesty, selflessness,* and *commitment* . . . of those who govern. . . . In practice, where the moralistic political culture is dominant today, there is considerably more *amateur participation* in politics.[24]

Elazar's characterization of this culture suggests a political environment potentially receptive to the values and style that have traditionally been associated with women—concern with the public welfare rather than personal enrichment and so forth. In addition, during the early 1950s Arizona had a relatively high seats ratio (10 per 100,000 persons), a structural feature shown to be a basic precondition for the election of women legislators. Heavy immigration throughout the 1950s and 1960s and the reduction in the size of the legislature in 1967 lowered the seats ratio considerably (to 3 per 100,000 in the 1971 session), but the proportion of women legislators did not fall. This seems to follow the pattern found in Connecticut: when initial conditions create an environment favorable to the election of women legislators, women will continue to be elected even when those conditions change. In Arizona much of the population growth was due to the influx of retired persons—persons less likely to compete for political office—and so the growth of population in terms of potential competitors for seats was somewhat less than the actual population growth.[25]

The moralistic political culture is not unique to Arizona. According to Elazar it is rather strong in the Far West, the Northwest, and New England. Of these regions only New England has a high proportion of women legislators, and according to Elazar the only New England states in which the moralistic strain is not part of the dominant culture are Rhode Island and Massachusetts—the two deviants. The moralistic political culture was probably responsible for the original establishment of the large citizen legislatures throughout New England, but by the time women acquired the vote and began running for public office the moralistic culture had given way to the individualistic culture in the areas that became heavily industrialized and populated by European immigrants.[26]

But is the dominance of the moralistic culture a necessary condition for the recruitment and election of women legislators? On the basis of Elazar's categorization there are many states with a strong moralistic strain that do not have a high proportion of women legislators. It is striking, however, that over time the states that have tended to elect the highest proportions of women legislators, excluding the New England "vanguard," have been Arizona, Washington, Oregon, and Colorado, states where the moralistic strain presumably has been dominant. This culture certainly is not a sufficient condition for the recruitment and election of women legislators, but it may be a necessary condition. With its emphasis on communitarianism and citizen participation by all, it contrasts with the traditionalistic and the individualistic political cultures.

> The traditionalistic political culture . . . accepts a substantially hierarchial society as part of the ordered nature of things, authorizing and expecting those at the top of the social structure to take a special and dominant role in government.

> [The individualistic political culture] emphasizes the conception of the democratic order as a marketplace. . . . it holds politics to be just another means by which individuals may improve themselves. . . . politics is a "business" like any other that competes for talent and offers rewards to those who take it up as a career.

The traditionalistic political culture—primarily a southern phenomenon—with its emphasis on elite participation in politics, is not likely to favor the participation of women, and, in fact, the southern states have elected very few women legislators. The individualistic political culture, with its emphasis on politics as "business," looks upon political activity as essentially

> the province of professionals. . . . There is a strong tendency among the public to believe that politics is a dirty—if necessary—business, better left to those who are willing to soil themselves by engaging in it.[27]

Competitive, professional, and sometimes even ruthless politics are not likely to provide favorable conditions for the participation of women.

Refinement of the Model

The equation which confirmed that the proportion of women in the lower house is inversely related to competition for lower house seats was based on data from a particular time—1971. Closer examination of the data indicated the importance of historical precedents and cultural history in explaining the contemporary pattern. A state may not have especially favorable structural conditions today, but it may have had them at some earlier point, and patterns established in an earlier period will persist even when structural conditions change. And, in fact, the history of competition for seats—competition for seats averaged over time—is a more powerful predictor than data for any one session. Seats per 100,000 persons averaged over the period 1950–70 explains 31 percent of the variation in the proportion of women in lower houses in 1971. But also important is the sheer fact that women may have entered a political arena in the past. After the first woman has been elected from a district, it is likely to be somewhat easier for those who follow. Women have a better chance to be elected to the senate in states where substantial numbers have been elected to the house. The best single predictor of where women are today is where they were yesterday: the proportion of women in state houses in 1961 explains 37 percent of the variation in 1971. Building from this we find that a model which includes as explanatory variables both the 1961 pattern of representation and the competition-for-seats ratio over time accounts for 49 percent of the variation in the contemporary pattern (see appendix 7).

When women break barriers, a certain cultural milieu is created which eases further entry. But can the characteristics of a favorable milieu be identified? Daniel Elazar's discussion of political subcultures is suggestive; but unfortunately, since his concepts are derived from subjective judgments, they do not permit precise quantitative specification of the relevant aspects of culture.[28]

The analysis also indicated that southern legislatures have consistently had fewer women than other regions. If a dummy variable for the South is included in the multivariate model, we can then explain 54 percent of the variation in the proportion of women legislators. But this southern location variable, like all such regional variables, does not indicate a specific reason for fewer women legislators in the South. Elazar's notion of a traditionalistic political culture is intuitively compelling, but that explanation may amount to no more than a simple assertion that the South is inhospitable for women seeking political office.[29]

Impact of the Women's Movement

By 1974 the subject of women's liberation was no longer confined to a few cell units within the New Left. The women's movement had evolved into a visible social phenomenon encompassing groups and individuals across the political spectrum. Profound cultural changes were in the making. The influence of these changes on the relationships we have identified from the era before the full development of the women's movement constitutes a topic in its own right.[30]

The returns from the 1974 elections showed that more women than ever before would be serving in American state legislatures. Women now constituted 9.1 percent of the legislators in lower houses and 5 percent of the legislators in upper houses. They were still very far from achieving political parity, but in the four-year interval their representation doubled. Except for the election year immediately succeeding the winning of women's suffrage, no change of this magnitude has ever occurred in such a short time.

And yet if the overall pattern of differences among the states is examined, it looks much the same as ever (see appendix 2). In the 1975 session deviant New Hampshire was still far out in front, with 102 women in the house. The New England "vanguard" states were still the only states with more than 20 female legislators. There is a very strong relationship between the proportion of women in 1971 and the proportion in 1975 ($r = .80$). And, significantly, the model developed for 1971 also explains the 1975 pattern (see appendix 7). But considering that the explanatory power of this model stems from the continuity of traditions, extraordinary events would have had to take place for previous patterns to disappear. It is more appropriate to ask where marked shifts from the basic pattern did occur and whether there is an apparent explanation for such shifts.

Before such changes in lower house patterns are examined, a development in state senates warrants attention: the vast majority of women senators in 1975 had not previously served in the lower houses. Of the 91 serving in this session, 77 were directly elected to the senate, while only 14 had traveled the house-to-senate route—a mere 15 percent as opposed to 60 percent in 1971. But as in previous sessions, the upper house pattern is related to the lower house pattern ($r = .62$); successful senate candidacies are still related to successful house candidacies. The most visible change is that female state senators are considerably more common: in 1971, 23 states had no female senators, in 1975 only 8. Most states now have their token female senator, but the average number per chamber is still only 1.8.[31]

The scatterplot in figure 2.3 plots each state's 1975 proportion of women legislators against its 1971 proportion. It illustrates the persistence of the overall pattern from 1971 to 1975: most states with high proportions in 1971 retained these high proportions in 1975, while those with low proportions continued to be low. In addition we can see the overall growth which occurred

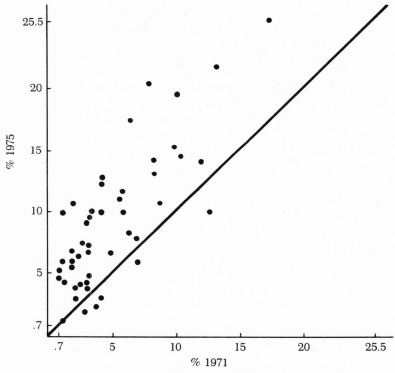

Figure 2.3   Percentage of Women in House in 1975, by Percentage in 1971

during this period: most states lie *above* the 45° line, indicating that most legislatures have a higher proportion of women in 1975 than they did in 1971. The average shift was an increase of 4.2 percent. In order to detect any emerging patterns it would be important to know if the states that deviated noticeably from this average shift held anything in common. The ten states which had increases of more than 6 percent are identified in table 2.2. They are a diverse group: every region is represented and the states vary considerably in land area and population size, as well as in socioeconomic development and political patterns. Two southern states—Florida and North Carolina—were among those with high proportions of change, and in fact Alabama, Arkansas, Louisiana, and Mississippi were the only southern states that lagged considerably behind the national growth rate. By 1975 the South was no longer a distinct region with respect to the underrepresentation of women. The best explanatory model for the overall pattern in 1975 is one which does not include the South as a separate variable.[32]

Table 2.2 Changes in Female Representation in Top Ten Lower
Houses from 1971 Session to 1975 Session

	1971 Session (%)	1975 Session (%)	Absolute Change (%)
Colorado	7.7	20.0	12.3
Delaware	10.0	19.3	9.3
North Carolina	1.7	10.8	9.1
Montana	1.0	10.0	9.0
North Dakota	4.0	12.7	8.7
Idaho	4.3	12.9	8.6
Arizona	13.3	21.7	8.4
New Hampshire	17.3	25.5	8.2
Florida	3.4	10.0	6.6
Wyoming	3.3	9.7	6.4

Neither the absolute nor the relative changes in the proportions of female legislators during this four-year interval reveals any new structural relationships. Reasoning that only in highly populated states would there be a sufficiently large base for women's movement activities to have spin-offs in electoral politics, I had expected a positive association between increases in the proportion of female legislators and population size, while actually the reverse occurred ($r = -.35$); growth was greater in the less populated states. The overall growth during this period was probably a consequence of the visibility of the women's issue in the early 1970s, but if this development is to have an impact on the relative differences among the states it is too early to tell how this will come about.[33]

This analysis has increased our understanding of why women have been more regularly elected in certain places than in others. Though no specific, foolproof strategy for electing more women to state legislatures can be generated from findings such as these, two very general approaches can be suggested.

Where favorable conditions exist more women are likely to be elected if more women run. During the four-year interval the *largest* increase in the *number* of female legislators (68 to 102) took place in New Hampshire; the *largest relative* increase in the *proportion* of female legislators (an increase of 939 percent—from .96 percent to 10 percent) occurred in Montana, a state that previously had fewer women than predicted on the basis of its competition-for-seats ratio.* However, there are few states with favorable competition-for-seats ratios, and it is unlikely that the number will increase. The trend in recent years has been to reduce the size of legislatures, and, given the orientation of groups that concern themselves with legislative effectiveness, this will probably continue. In addition, population size in most states will increase rather than decrease. Women are also likely to succeed where women legislators have been elected frequently in the past. Colorado had the largest *absolute* increase (12.3 percentage points) in the *proportion* of female legislators, and this is a state that has long been relatively advanced in terms of female political equality. It was one of the earliest states to grant women suffrage and in 1921 had four women in its legislature—second only to Connecticut.[34]

But if women are to be elected in states where these favorable conditions do not exist, new conditions will have to be created. The individualistic political culture is strong in all the heavily populated urban states, and here political participation demands professionalism and competition. Unless women choose to concentrate their efforts on changing this dominant political tradition (and many would argue for this general approach), they will have to develop the organizational skills that the individualistic political culture demands. If the choice is to win within this culture, another dilemma arises. Other groups in such states are likely to be highly organized: should women integrate

---

* Montana had the largest negative residual for the 1971 equation.

(or infiltrate?) these entrenched groups or should they develop their own organizations? Other minorities have generally chosen to create their own pressure groups while at the same time working within more established political organizations. But women are not a statistical minority, and they are the only political minority in which the majority of the group lives in intimate contact with the political majority.

In considering strategies it may prove valuable to look back to the women's movement at the turn of the century. After women gained the vote in 1920, there was little support for maintaining a feminist organization to concentrate on women's rights issues. Emily Newell Blair was one suffrage leader who rejected the "sex-conscious feminists" of the Woman's Party and advocated that women work within the existing political parties. She herself was the first woman to become national vice-chairman of the Democratic party. However, at the end of the decade Blair's optimism about achieving equality had faded, and she called for a revival of feminist organizations. In refutation of her own earlier position she wrote in 1931: "Unfortunately for feminism it was agreed to drop the sex line in politics." She argued that women could not bring power to politics and command respect unless they had a following.[35]

3: Sex Differences in Four New England Legislatures

This chapter examines the behavioral differences of female and male legislators and the effects that competition for office has on these differences. The legislatures of Connecticut, Maine, New Hampshire, and Vermont will provide the focus of study. Although these four legislatures certainly differ in many respects—the existence of "two New Englands" has often been remarked upon—the similarities among them in terms of their institutional development and current practices are, when contrasted with other state legislatures, compelling. As chapter 2 showed, Connecticut, Maine, New Hampshire, and Vermont are all states where, historically, seat competition has been relatively mild. In effect this chapter will detail sex differences at one end of the spectrum simply because at the other end the number of women is minuscule and hence provides no basis for systematic study.

But such an examination, which is for the most part a simple description, is not as limited as at first glance it might appear to be. The discussion up to now has treated the state as the unit of analysis: states have been said to have either competitive or noncompetitive systems. But recruitment to the legislature, though certainly shaped by the state political system, takes place within individual districts. James Barber, who studied the Connecticut legislature when that body was a citizen legislature to an even greater extent than it is today, found that the characteristics of the district affected the recruitment process markedly.

> In very many of the small towns of Connecticut the major problem for the local party committee is not resolving fac-

tional contests over nominations, but simply finding some minimally acceptable person to allow his name to be put on the ballot. . . . The problem is one of "Who is available?" rather than "Which of these contestants should we favor?" [1]

The party recruiter is forced to become fairly nonselective, and consequently he actively encourages the participation of the politically inexperienced. Barber found that legislators who achieved their positions in this way participated minimally in legislative activities and had limited political ambitions. These "Spectators," as he called them, were frequently retired persons and women.

Thus, on the basis of Barber's findings, we might expect that in districts where the availability of suitable candidates was a problem—where seat competition was negligible—women would be more highly represented than in districts with significant competition for seats. Women from competitive districts could also be expected to be fairly similar to their male counterparts with respect to their political careers and legislative behavior.

Matters of Method

There are inherent difficulties in generalizing about sex differences on the basis of these four states. Though historically they have shared many characteristics—social, economic, and constitutional—they still differ in certain ways. There are variations in the strength of party organizations and in the degree of party competition, and also differences in political culture. The attempt to get on with the overdue examination of sex differences among political leaders has of late given rise to a tendency to pool together, for analysis, leaders from disparate backgrounds.[2] Care must be taken, however, that differences attributed to sex are not merely the result of institutional differences. Another problem is that sex differences in one context—in this study, a state—may be cancelled by sex differences in the opposite direction in another context. For example, in state A men may be more active than women, while in state B women are more active than men, with an aggregate result indicating no sex difference. To guard against this possibility I have performed all major calculations within each state.

The data were obtained through a questionnaire mailed in December 1971 to all female state legislators in Connecticut, Maine, New Hampshire, and Vermont, and to a selected sample of male legislators in these states. Each man was selected to match a woman with the same party affiliation residing in the same town or, where this was not possible, in an adjoining town with comparable population in the same county. Republicans cooperated with considerably greater frequency than Democrats (see appendix 3). The differential response rates raise certain problems of bias. The nonrespondents were more heavily Democratic than the respondents. The percentage of women legislators in these four states who were Democrats was 33 percent, whereas among the female respondents the proportion of Democrats was 26 percent. This means that if Democratic women differ from Democratic men to a greater extent than Republican women differ from Republican men, the overall sex differences reported will be smaller than they are in the actual population; conversely, if sex differences among Democrats are smaller than those among Republicans, the overall differences reported here will be exaggerated. But as the overall party breakdowns among male respondents and female respondents were roughly similar, I can be confident that reported sex differences do indeed point to sex differences and are not masking party differences.

First of all, we shall look into sex differences with respect to (1) socialization to politics; (2) social and economic origins; (3) political careers; and (4) legislative behavior. This should show the extent to which there is a female pattern that differs from the male pattern. But after the documenting of differences— and the available literature suggests that sex differences among political elites tend to reflect differences in the general population [3]—our concern will shift to factors that modify sex contrasts. Identification of these factors is crucial if we are to explore what sex differences might look like in the future.

Political Socialization

"Men are being 'selected' for office years before their first campaign or initial victory. The experiences which direct citizens toward a career in public life are often removed by decades and by great distances from the office they actually hold." [4] Men as a class—particularly those with high socioeconomic status—are "selected"; women as a class are not "selected." Studies of young children from the earliest years show that girls exhibit a lower interest in and awareness of politics than their male peers.[5] The differing orientations do not flow mainly from a rational developmental sequence in which girls learn that "politics is not for girls," hence "I am not interested in politics." The process is more subtle. Young girls and boys are given differential opportunities for rewards and punishments—girls for passivity and submission, boys for aggressiveness and self-assertion. Children learn to apply society's standards to themselves and to other children. Identification with the appropriate sex models takes place at a young age; one study which presented films to children found that children tended to recall better the behavior of models of the same sex, especially when the models displayed appropriate sex-typed behavior.[6] Identification for a young boy means associations with the wider social, political, and economic environment; identification for a young girl means associations with home and family, and a relationship with the wider environment that is only marginal. Specific political responses, which evolve later in childhood, fall into the already developed framework of nonpolitical orientations.

Women who assume active political roles may be said to be "deviant" in terms of dominant social norms and expectations. How does their political socialization compare with that of their male peers? For both the male and female legislators in this study it was noticeable that the family was important in shaping initial interest in politics. This agrees with what the socialization literature and the numerous studies of political elites have shown.[7] However, as expected, the family was considerably more important for the women: 50 percent of the women listed "family" as important in getting them interested in politics, while only 23 percent of the men did so. It is also significant that only 7 percent of the women listed "job" as a factor in their initial interest, and only 4 percent listed "occupational ties" as leading to their active involvement; the comparable figures for the men are 16 percent and 20 percent. The importance of the occupational nexus has often been noted in studies of political leaders.[8] Certain occupations such as law and business tend to involve frequent contact with the public sector, and consequently individuals with these backgrounds are disproportionately represented among political leaders. Women are certainly a significant factor in the labor force—thirty-three million women were working in March 1972—but the largest numbers do service and clerical work, occupations which do not facilitate movement into public office.[9]

The study considered the question of whether the legislators came from political families. With respect to general political atmosphere in the childhood home, for legislators of both sexes the mother was not as "political" as the father. This fact simply reflects the basic division of family roles prevalent in the society at large. This division of roles was probably even more pronounced at the time these legislators were growing up; sex differences in general forms of political activity have been gradually eroding over the last fifty years.[10] Some of the legislators were being acculturated before women won the vote or shortly thereafter, which explains why many of the mothers never voted at all.

There are, however, important differences between the male and female legislators in the early home political atmosphere, particularly with respect to the mothers. The women came from families in which the political atmosphere was more intense: both the mothers and fathers were relatively active. The activity of the women's mothers contrasts sharply with that of the men's mothers; for example, 45 percent of the women's mothers discussed politics frequently, while among the men the figure is only 21 percent.

Differences between the sexes with respect to the elite political participation of parents are not marked. Few legislators had parents or relatives who held office. But here again activity reflects general societal patterns: fathers and male relatives more commonly held office than mothers and female relatives. It is possibly significant, however, that the five office-holding mothers of the women held political offices, whereas the three office-holding mothers of the men all served as board of education members. Moreover, the office-holding relatives of the females included an aunt and a grandmother, while in the case of the male legislators such relatives were all men.

Mothers may have served as positive role models for some of the female legislators. The data support the argument that the family experience is more critical for the political activation of women than of men. Although the role of the family certainly should not be minimized in the latter case, in a male-dominated society men are more likely to be exposed to political cues in the world outside the family. In some sense, then, they can compensate for what they missed in the family, as other opportunities are likely to present themselves. Women, on the other hand, need strong political cues within the family to drown out or at least modify the cues they receive from the wider environment. As basic values and behavior patterns are learned early in life, it is crucial that a female be exposed to political matters during this formative period, within the intimacy of the family. A woman is unlikely to become active in politics if exposure to political matters occurs only later in life, for such activity would typically conflict with the pattern already learned. A man experiences no such lack of congruence and may readily become politically active during an advanced phase of his adult career. Political activity for a man is not likely to be disruptive of his basic life-pattern. And of course a man often enters political office from a career in the wider environment—such as business or law—where he has developed certain skills that can be transferred to politics.

Up to now I have been arguing for the importance of the natal family in the political socialization of females. But differences in incidence of spouse involvement attest to the importance of the adult nuclear family for female legislators. Thirty-five percent of the women's husbands hold party or public office as compared to only 13 percent of the men's wives. It is also interesting that incidence of spouse involvement is greater among housewives than among employed women: 41 percent of the housewives had husbands who were involved as compared to 32 percent of the employed women. In their study of Michigan party delegates, Jennings and Thomas likewise found that the incidence of spouse involvement was greater among women, particularly housewives.[11] It could be argued that females who do not receive appropriate political socialization in their natal families can compensate somewhat for such deprivation by marrying politically active men. Politically active husbands can sometimes provide their wives with opportunities to enter public office. Widow's succession is the most clear-cut form of this manner of entry.

Socioeconomic Background

Distinct sex-related differences appear in the socioeconomic characteristics of the legislators. Occupation and employment status reflect the differing social roles of men and women. Forty-six percent of the women list their occupation as housewife, while 53 percent of the men hold jobs in either the professions or business. The vast majority of the women currently employed outside the home (several of those who listed housewife also listed other occupations) hold relatively low-status positions. Clerical and sales and service positions are the norm; none is an attorney; and only 5.3 percent are in the professions. Moreover, 67 percent of the men are self-employed, whereas this is true of only 22 percent of the working women. "When women work, they tend to do so for someone else; men are more independent economically, especially in an elite group." [12] Clearly there are important status differences between the sexes here; however, these male legislators are not a particularly elite group compared to legislators in many other states. [13] A very high proportion of the men are retired (32 percent), and only 12 percent are attorneys.

The age differences between the men and women also reflect societal sex roles. As expected, there are very few young women; only 7 percent of the women are under forty as compared to 21 percent of the men. Young children generally preclude only mothers, not fathers, from active political and occupational involvement. Twenty-eight percent of the men had a child below the age of ten, while this was true of only 13 percent of the women. The female legislators have not foregone childbearing for their political careers (twenty-eight had families with four or more children), for each of the sexes had an average of 2.6 children. Perhaps most striking is the fact that a large proportion of the legislators are elderly: 40 percent of the men and 31 percent of the women are sixty-five years old or more. Not surprisingly, this age pattern results in distinct differences with respect to marital status. Among men 89 percent are married and 4 percent are widowed, while among women 59 percent are married and 24 percent widowed. Widowhood may provide women with an opportunity for a new career.

Educational disparities between the sexes appear at the higher achievement levels (table 3.1). The majority of both sexes have not had any training beyond "some college"; however, women who continue generally stop with the college degree, whereas many men go on to obtain advanced degrees. The male legislator's occupational pattern often necessitates more educational preparation; the female legislator's occupation does not. (There is no difference in the educational achievement levels of employed and nonemployed women. [14])

The income differences between the sexes again reflect their social roles (table 3.2). [15] Fifty percent of the female legislators have *individual* incomes of less than $5,000 annually, while the

Table 3.1 Education, by Sex

	Female (%)	Male (%)
High school or less	43	40
Some college *	21	26
College degree	20	7
Some post-college	7	6
Advanced degree †	9	20
Totals	100	100
(N)	(76)	(108)

* includes nursing school and business college
† includes all law degrees

same is true of only 13 percent of the men. No women have *individual* incomes over $25,000, but 13 percent of the men are in this bracket. The disparity between individual and family incomes indicates several things: (1) many of the women are dependent on spouses for their support; (2) the men are not so dependent; and (3) women who support themselves are relatively poor. In contrast to two earlier studies which indicated that female political leaders come from lower economic strata than males, the sexes here do not appear to come from appreciably different levels.[16] The Jennings and Thomas study found that nonemployed women had higher family incomes than employed women, and this was found to be the case here also: 42 percent of the women at home had family incomes of $20,000 or over, as compared to 27 percent of the employed women.

Table 3.2 Income, by Sex

Annual Income ($)	Female (%)		Male (%)	
	Individual	Family	Individual	Family
Less than 4,999	50	11	13	10
5,000–9,999	34	23	33	24
10,000–14,999	10	11	17	22
15,000–19,999	3	19	19	19
20,000–24,999	3	13	6	6
25,000 and over		23	13	19
Totals	100	100	100	100
(N)	(62)	(53)	(102)	(95)

We come now to the relationship between sex, class, and political participation in these New England states. Jennings and Thomas argued on the basis of their data that upper-class women who participate in public affairs prefer nonpartisan to partisan activity in greater proportion than upper-class men. They found that for less affluent women, on the other hand, partisan activity is the major vehicle for involvement in public affairs, since such women have fewer opportunities than upper-class women to become involved in high-status civic and social organizations.[17] Our study of New England legislators lends no support to the first part of their argument; these women do not come from appreciably lower economic strata, and similar proportions of men and women have at least a college degree. The education and income data indicate that less privileged women are well represented in these legislatures, but so are less privileged men. As stated previously, these men are *relatively* non-elite legislators. Legislative activity is a vehicle for involvement in public affairs for the less privileged of both sexes. An upper-class background is not a necessary requirement for obtaining legislative office; in fact, there is a striking degree of variation in the backgrounds of these legislators. As expected, the requirements for legislative office are neither select nor specific, which explains the relatively high proportion of female legislators.

Political Careers

What is most impressive about the political histories of the legislators under study is that the aggregate differences between the sexes are not as great as one might have expected. Neither the women nor the men contemplated holding public office from their earliest years (table 3.3). Interest in public office generally arose during adulthood, and for many it was only in response to their being *asked* to run for office. A substantial number appear to have followed what Kenneth Prewitt, in a study of city councilmen, labelled "the pathway of lateral entry"—entrance into the stratum of politically active citizens by direct recruitment into public office.[18] Very few of the New England legislators

Table 3.3 Initial Interest in Position in Government, by Sex

	Female (%)	Male (%)
Childhood	3	5
Adolescence	3	12
Adulthood	58	47
When I was asked to run	57	39
(N)	(76)	(109)

have been preoccupied with politics throughout their lives. Their interest in politics generally developed during adulthood and grew out of community activities—by far the most common avenue to active involvement for both sexes (table 3.4). Their different social roles, however, are reflected in the fact that for women party ties were more important than occupational ties, whereas for men the reverse was true. It is noteworthy that occupational ties were equally unimportant for the employed and nonemployed women: as indicated earlier, very few of these women hold jobs which routinely provide contact with politics.

Table 3.4 Most Important Connection Leading to
Active Involvement in Politics, by Sex

	Female (%)	Male (%)
Community activities	73	67
Party ties	30	17
Occupational ties	4	20
(N)	(70)	(107)

The great majority of both sexes had some affiliation with partisan politics prior to becoming legislators (78 percent of the women and 73 percent of the men). But perhaps what is most significant is that one-fourth of these legislators had no involvement whatsoever. And for many what involvement they did have was fairly minor; only 46 percent of the men and 47 percent of the women held some party office. Sex differences do appear in the kinds of party activities engaged in. As expected, women are more active in the routine aspects of campaign

work, men in the nonroutine aspects: women usually distributed literature and contacted voters, while men made policy
decisions. There were, however, no differences with respect to
speech-making, and women were more active in managing
campaigns. The activity of women in campaign management
exceeded expectations, but it is very likely that managing local
campaigns in these states demands willingness to carry out
many routine tasks rather than sophisticated executive or decision-making skills.[19]

There are distinct sex differences in the kinds of party offices
held. These differences mirror the division of tasks in nonpolitical institutions: 25 percent of the women held the office of
"secretary," while only one male had this post; 30 percent of the
men held the office of "chairman," in contrast to 12 percent of
the women, and all the female chairmanships were at the pre-
cinct or municipal levels; 14 percent of the women held the office of "vice-chairman," while only four men held this office.
Only the office of "supervisor of the check list," a New England
election-board position, was not dominated by either sex. The
majority of the offices held by both sexes were at the local level,
neither sex being appreciably more active at county or state
levels.

In contrast to the findings of Jennings and Thomas, men and
women were equally likely to hold either elective or appointive
public office.[20] Approximately one-third of both the women and
the men had held neither elective nor appointive public office
prior to assuming legislative duties. But once again differences
appear in the kinds of offices held. A position on the local school
board was the most common elective office among women (18
percent), while a position on the city council was the most common among men (26 percent). However, neither of these positions was exclusively female or male, for 12 percent of the
males served on school boards and 12 percent of the females on
city councils. These legislators served in a variety of local elective offices: library trustee and town clerk were typical for
women; justice of the peace and town moderator (honorary

chairperson of New England town meetings) were typical for men.

The immediate circumstances leading to the legislative career provide another area in which to look for distinct sex-related patterns. The vast majority of both sexes gained office at regular elections, and neither the women nor the men who were elected at special elections (6 women, 4 men) were filling the seats of spouses. The men, however, were more likely to have sought office on their own initiative (table 3.5). Here again what is perhaps most noteworthy is the fact that large numbers of both the women and the men had to be persuaded to run.

Table 3.5 Circumstances Leading to First Campaign for the Legislature, by Sex

	Female (%)	Male (%)
Sought office	16	29
Sought office, but had encouragement from party	18	20
Sought office, but had encouragement from community groups	28	25
Did not seek office	43	31
(N)	(75)	(105)

Despite the fact that men were more likely to seek office on their own—an expected finding—the sexes did not differ at all in the amount of opposition they faced for their nomination. These findings might appear to contradict each other, but perhaps they indicate that, though women may be less likely to reach a decision to seek office on their own, once they make that decision they are as willing to face opposition as men. This matter is in need of further exploration.

Once elected, women and men do not appear to differ appreciably in the degree of commitment to the legislative career; if anything, the women may be slightly more committed. The women under study had served an average of seven years in the legislature, and 30 percent were willing to serve three or more terms, while the corresponding figures for the men were six years and 22 percent. Differences in career commitment reappear with respect to progressive political ambitions. Forty-five percent of the men were interested in seeking other political or government positions, while this is true of only 18 percent of the women. What ambitions the women did have were fairly limited: most typical was an interest in being a committee chairman or state senator; only five women indicated an interest in statewide office. In contrast, men with progressive political ambitions were frequently interested in state-wide office. Not one woman aspired to an executive position, whereas several men were interested in being governor or even president.

These data confirm what was already quite apparent, that fewer women than men seek public office; but they also indicate that once women achieve office they are just as interested in maintaining their position as men are.

It was predicted that women legislators would be more common in districts where the availability of suitable candidates was a problem. And in fact the women tend to represent districts in which little change has occurred in the social or ethnic composition of the population: [21] 79 percent of the women indicated that their district's population had either "changed somewhat" or "changed not at all," while 66 percent of the men represented such districts. In Barber's Connecticut study, availability of suitable candidates was a problem not only in districts where little population change had occurred, but in rural small towns as well. Among the New England legislators approximately one-half of both the women and men came from districts in which rural communities and small towns predominated, and the sexes did not differ appreciably in terms of the population of their districts. But this is not surprising in view of the reapportionment changes of the mid-sixties which reduced representational disparities between rural and nonrural areas.

Surprisingly similar proportions of women and men came from "competitive" districts, but this may be explained by the apparent unwillingness of the Democrats to nominate women when the seat is relatively safe. Among the Democratic women a minority came from Democratic districts, while among the Democratic men the large majority did.[22] The historical analysis of the previous chapter indicated that, for women, Republican areas have traditionally been more favorable than Democratic areas, and our data suggest that this is still the case today. The more favorable competition-for-seats ratio in rural Republican districts no longer obtains, but these earlier conditions established precedents that influence recruitment today—21 percent of the women came from "safe Republican" districts, while this was true of 12 percent of the men.

Legislative Behavior

Are there distinct female and male modes of adjusting to the legislative environment? Traditional social roles appear to have an important influence on the "niches" women and men develop—the policy areas they specialize in and the leadership posts they hold—but beyond this, the behavioral and attitudinal differences are not substantial.

The sexes develop different areas of policy expertise. Women most frequently cited "Education" (18 percent) as their area of expertise, while men cited "Fiscal Affairs" (17 percent). However, Education was also frequently specified by the men (8 percent). It should be recalled that many of the men as well as the women served on school boards prior to entering the legislature. Health and Welfare was the second most frequent area among the women (8 percent). There were no other areas frequently mentioned by either sex.

Not surprisingly, women's areas of expertise are reflected in the committees they serve on. Women were concentrated on two committees: 26 percent served on Health and Welfare, and 25 percent on Education. Men, being the majority, were not concentrated in any particular committees. Unanticipated was the finding that 20 percent of the women serve on Agriculture. Perhaps this is explained by the fact that many of the legislators rated Agriculture as only "somewhat important." Women, however, did not appear to be excluded from the important committees; 14 percent served on Judiciary and 11 percent on Ways and Means. Though women are not excluded from the important committees, still we cannot determine from these data that discrimination is not present. Differences between legislatures are probably very important here. Chapter 5 deals with some of these differences with respect to the allocation of chairmanships.

As expected, important leadership positions are more commonly held by the men. The respondents were asked to specify what leadership positions they held currently or had held in the past. Three women had held the post of assistant minority leader and one the post of caucus secretary. The men had held the following offices—President of the Senate, Majority Leader (3), Minority Leader (2), Assistant Minority Leader (2), and Whip (5). Considering that there are no differences between the sexes in length of tenure, sex is clearly an important criterion for the allocation of leadership positions.

For the purpose of determining legislative participation, the respondents were asked how frequently they had taken part in a variety of legislative activities. A participation scale based on self-reporting has some significant limitations. I have made the assumption (or leap of faith) that the self-reporting was not systematically biased along sex lines. Three of the items—"speak on floor," "question witnesses," and "take an active part in major negotiations"—allow us to construct an "activity scale" (see appendix 4 for further details).

On the basis of the activity scale males are slightly more active than females.* This finding was as expected: males more often hold leadership positions, and the aspects of activity measured by this scale all require somewhat assertive behavior. Females, however, more frequently introduced bills (gamma = .10) and spoke in executive sessions of committees (gamma = .37). Introducing bills does not necessitate assertive behavior; it may require some background research, but traditional sex-role socialization normally does not hinder women in this respect. Introducing bills is also the legislative activity most likely to be no-

---

* The gamma correlation between sex (scoring males "0" and females "1") and activity is −.25. A positive gamma correlation means that women scored higher, while a negative correlation means that men scored higher.

ticed by constituents, and as demonstrated earlier these women are as interested in retaining their seats as the men. Similarly, speaking in executive sessions of committees does not require exceptionally assertive behavior; it is a much less formalized activity than speaking on the floor, and, as will be shown in the next chapter, many women simply feel more comfortable about speaking in committee than on the floor (the 400 seat house in New Hampshire is very large). Despite their greater participation in committee deliberations as speakers, women do not influence such deliberations as frequently as men (gamma $= -.22$). This disparity (between speaking and influence) may reflect accurate reporting: males hold more positions of legislative authority and have somewhat greater policy expertise, each of which can be a source of influence; and, moreover, conventional social roles lead females to accede and males to dominate. Any or all of these factors could account for the greater influence of men, but this may be an instance where the self-effacing attitudes engendered by traditional sex-role socialization have "distorted" the actual situation.

It was expected that women would be more averse to legislative bargaining than men. Women are generally presumed to be the more moralistic sex, and moralistic attitudes should lead to negative reactions to bargaining. The following three questionnaire items, designed to tap attitudes toward bargaining, formed a scale (see appendix 4):

1. Legislative vote-swapping is morally objectionable and should be avoided in the legislature.
2. The public would be better served if there were no bargaining in the legislature.
3. Find it necessary to trade votes with other legislators.

Women did score lower on the bargaining scale; women are more negatively disposed toward bargaining than are men. Women were also somewhat more likely to agree with the following statements: "Lobbyists and special interests have entirely too much influence in American state legislatures," and "With his better sources of information a legislator should vote as he thinks best even when his constituents disagree." Neither of these statements was related to the bargaining dimension; but if we assume that these statements are tapping other aspects of moralism, then additional evidence is provided for the presumed moralistic orientation of women. We saw in chapter 2 that women are somewhat more likely to be elected where a moralistic political culture is dominant, and here, on the individual level, women showed themselves to be more likely to hold moralistic orientations.*

Whether or not these two items are measuring moralism, the relationships do indicate that women are somewhat more negatively disposed toward lobbyists and more inclined to adopt a "trustee" or Burkean stance with respect to constituents. Jennings and Thomas, however, found that among party delegates males had a much stronger Burkean orientation than females. They attributed this to

> the greater degree of independence and self-reliance which men enjoy in society and politics. Men are more accustomed to making their own decisions in nonpolitical as well as political matters. Women tend to be less self-sufficient and to seek certainty and assurance in people, institutions, and concepts outside themselves. Consequently, *men rely more heavily on their own judgment as a guide to decision on party matters* than do female counterparts.[23]

Women may very well be less self-reliant in their manner of making decisions—among these legislators men indicated a slightly greater degree of independence with respect to legislative decision-making [24]—but the Burkean orientation refers to the legislator's mode of ascertaining what is in the best interest of constituents, not to party decision-making. A Burkean posture might lead a legislator to vote contrary to the "expressed" wishes of constituents if the legislator felt that these wishes were at odds with the constituents' true interests. Women, being

---

* The gamma correlation between sex and bargaining (scoring positive attitude "high") was −.38. Scoring agreement "low," the gamma between sex and lobbyists was −.25; gamma between sex and information was −.28.

less politically ambitious, might be expected to feel freer to vote in such a fashion.[25] This was a sentiment expressed by several of the women legislators who were interviewed.

Women had slightly more "liberal" policy views in all the issue areas that were examined. As measured by scores on a question concerning the best means of discouraging riots and disorders, women were more likely to emphasize solving the problems of poverty while men more often stressed using all

Table 3.6 Views on Day Care, by Sex

	Females (%)	Males (%)
No services	4	13
Only for welfare families if family working	25	36
For all, each paying what he can afford	68	47
Free for all	3	4
Totals	100	100
(N)	(72)	(101)

Table 3.7 Views on State Labor Laws, by Sex

	Females (%)	Males (%)
Benefit women today	56	75
In between	13	3
Do not benefit women today	31	22
Totals	100	100
(N)	(70)	(103)

available force (gamma = .28). Women tended to be more generous with regard to the provision of day-care services (table 3.6). The clear majority of women were in favor of the provision of day-care services for all who desire it, while almost one-half of the males preferred limited services. Both sexes were inclined to think that state labor laws designed to protect the interests of women did benefit women today, but there was greater agreement on this among the men than among the women (table 3.7). In the questionnaire the legislators were offered only the choices of "benefit" and "do not benefit": 13 percent of the women revised the question to indicate that their views fell between these two positions, while only 3 percent of the men so revised the question. This suggests that the women may have given some greater thought to the issue, which is indeed of more immediate concern to women.

On the question of abortion (table 3.8) the majority of women felt that the abortion law in their state should be repealed, while the majority of the men took a more moderate position. However, women and men were equally likely to take the antiabor-

Table 3.8 Views on Abortion, by Sex and Religion

			Catholic		Non-Catholic	
	Females %	Males %	Females %	Males %	Females %	Males %
The abortion law should be reformed so that it will be *harder* to obtain a legal abortion	9	7	38	6	2	6
No changes are needed	20	34	50	71	13	14
The abortion law should be reformed so that it will be *easier* to obtain a legal abortion	15	23	6	9	16	31
The abortion law should be repealed so that abortion will be a private matter between doctor and patient	56	35	6	15	70	49
Totals	100	100	100	101	101	100
(N)	(75)	(105)	(16)	(34)	(56)	(65)
	Gamma = .25		Gamma = − .57		Gamma = .34	

tion position. Interestingly, among the Catholic legislators women were considerably more negatively disposed toward abortion than men, whereas among non-Catholic legislators women were somewhat more favorably disposed than men. It is likely that if the proportion of female Catholic legislators were equal to the proportion of male Catholic legislators (22 percent of the females were Catholic, 33 percent of the males), the antiabortion stance would be even more common. Women are often said to be preservers of traditional religious values, and this appeared to be the case here. In fact the smaller percentage of Catholic women may be attributable to the more traditional attitudes about the proper role of women among Catholics. A female legislator interviewed in New Hampshire felt that in certain French Canadian Catholic districts women were very strongly discouraged from running.

Competition and Behavioral Differences

There are certain aspects of the recruitment practice which modify or accentuate the basic differences between female and male patterns. Figure 3.1 shows the central relationships; for each variable there are several indicators that bear examination.

Figure 3.1   Recruitment and Legislative Behavior

The primary indicators of seat competition are extent of opposition for the nomination, method of recruitment (seeking office or being asked to run), and degree of change in the composition of the district's population.[26] The primary indicators of occupation for men are simply "retired" and "currently employed," while for women they are "housewife" and "employed." Unfortunately so few women are professionals that it is not feasible to compare female and male professionals. Interest in higher office, public and party offices held, and involvement in party politics are the primary indicators of political career. And the primary indicators of legislative behavior are activity and bargaining.

What difference does seat competition make? If the male legislator had some opposition for the nomination he is less likely to be retired (29 percent of the males who had opposition were retired as opposed to 48 percent of those who had little or no opposition). Similarly, a female legislator who had some opposition is less likely to be a housewife (37 percent of the women who had opposition were housewives as opposed to 48 percent of those who had little or no opposition). Similar patterns appear in the method of recruitment: 30 percent of the men who sought office were retired as opposed to 52 percent of those asked to run; 37 percent of the females who sought office were housewives as opposed to 44 percent of those asked to run. Occupation, however, did not appear to be related in this same fashion to change in the district's population: the proportion of housewives in districts which had experienced considerable change was twice that of districts which had experienced little change, and the proportion of retired males was actually somewhat greater in the "change districts." Occupational background may not be related to population change in the expected direction, or these results may have been an artifact of the small number of cases involved. It will be recalled that, as predicted, a very small proportion of women came from "change" districts; the proportion of men was higher, but the actual number was still only thirty-five. I suspect that because the original hypothesis was borne out with respect to the proportion of women, the results here were due to the problems of introducing controls when the sample size is small.

As expected, political careers were related to seat competition. Both sexes were more likely to have been involved in party politics and to have held a party office when they sought their seat.[27] Similarly, both sexes were more interested in other offices when they sought their legislative seat. But as table 3.9 indicates, the differences between the sexes are not modified by the method of recruitment—men are considerably more interested in higher office in both cases. Sex is relevant to political ambitions then, but of greater significance is the fact that method of recruitment is still the more powerful explanatory variable for each facet of the political career considered—*differences between the sexes are less than differences be-*

Table 3.9 Interest in Higher Office, by Sex and Method of Recruitment

| | | Sought Office | | Asked to Run | |
		Female %	Male %	Female %	Male %
Interest in } No		74	45	90	75
Higher Office} Yes		26	55	10	25
Totals		100	100	100	100
(N)		(42)	(73)	(31)	(32)
		Gamma = −.55		Gamma = −.51	

tween methods of recruitment. And finally, for both sexes legislators who sought their seat were no more likely to have held public office, either appointive or elective, than legislators who were asked to run. It appears that party career most clearly distinguishes legislators who sought their seat from those who did not.

Opposition for the nomination has a differential impact on political careers. Only women were more likely to be involved in party politics and to have held party office when they had opposition for the nomination. Effectively the differences between the sexes are reversed with opposition: when there is little opposition for the nomination, men are more frequently involved in party politics and more frequently hold party offices; when there is much opposition for the nomination, women have the edge. (Table 3.10 indicates what occurs with respect to party offices.) On the other hand it was only men who had had opposition for the nomination who were more interested in higher office; women who had faced opposition had no greater political

Table 3.10 Party Office, by Sex and Opposition for Nomination

| | Little Opposition | | Much Opposition | |
	Female %	Male %	Female %	Male %
Did not hold office	61	44	44	67
Held office	40	56	56	33
Totals	100	100	100	100
(N)	(43)	(63)	(32)	(42)
	Gamma = −.31		Gamma = .44	

ambitions than those who had not. Differences in ambition between the sexes were even greater in the more competitive situation.*

The relationship between change in the composition of the
district's population and patterns of political career is not clear-
cut. This aspect of competition may not be as relevant as was
originally hypothesized, or these results may again be an artifact
of the samll number of cases involved. Among legislators who
came from districts in which there had been little change in the
composition of the district's population, there were no differences between the sexes with respect to prior involvement in
party politics or party offices held. In contrast, among legislators
who came from "change" districts, women were considerably
more   likely   to   have   been   involved   in   party   politics
(gamma = .45) and somewhat more likely to have held party office (gamma = .18). Once again competition seems to be of
greater consequence for the prior political involvements of
women. In contrast to the other aspects of competition that
have been considered here, interest in higher office does not
increase for men in the more competitive situation—36 percent
of those in "change" districts are interested in higher office,
while this is true of 50 percent of the men in the "no change"
districts. Political ambitions are in part a response to perceived
opportunities: there are probably many more potential aspirants
in "change" districts, which means that actual opportunities are
fewer. Hence the smaller proportion of current legislators interested in higher office.

Occupational status was shown to be related to two aspects of
seat competition. Is it in turn related to political careers and legislative behavior? The prelegislative political careers of the employed women were considerably more extensive than those of
the housewives. In fact it was the employed women who had
the bulk—63 percent—of party offices held by women. Compar-

* The gamma correlation between sex and interest in higher office for legislators who faced little or no opposition was −.31, while among those who faced
some or very much opposition it was −.70.

ing the two groups, 67 percent of the employed women held a party office while only 35 percent of the housewives did so. The employed women also were more likely to have held public office, both elective and appointive (table 3.11). Jennings and Thomas similarly found the employed women compared to housewives were more likely to compete for and hold office.[28] Since few of the employed women in either study had occupations that routinely provide contact with politics, it seems plausible that the differences between the two groups of women were largely due to personality and not to the opportunities of

Table 3.11 Correlations between Sex, Political Career, and
Legislative Behavior, by Employment Status

	Party Office	Appointed Office	Higher Office	Activity	Bargaining
Women—employed versus housewife	.57	.36	.16	.23	.00
Men—employed versus retired	.07	.10	.57	.37	.31

Note: In these gamma correlations a positive correlation indicates that employed women score higher than housewives and employed men score higher than retired men.

employment per se. Perhaps women with certain personality characteristics seek employment and these same characteristics propel them into politics; or perhaps the activity of employment outside the home promotes the development of these characteristics. It is also striking that despite their more extensive political involvements the employed women were not much more interested in higher office than the housewives (table 3.11). Though employed, they did not have professional careers, and thus lacked the skills and advantages that would make progressive political ambitions realistic.

We can turn now to legislative behavior. Here the data indicated that employed women were somewhat more active than housewives: 21 percent of the employed women scored at the highest activity level, while this was true of only 11 percent of the housewives. Employed women were therefore more similar to men, but only with respect to activity: on the bargaining index there were no differences between employed women and housewives (table 3.11). The sex-bargaining relationship, which was stronger than the sex-activity relationship, appears less subject to modification. The content of these women's jobs may again be relevant—a bookkeeper need not develop the negotiating skills which are a necessity for a lawyer or business-man—and therefore traditional feminine attitudes maintain themselves. But any employment outside the home generally involves an ability to manage more extensive commitments—the employed women had more active political careers prior to ob-

Table 3.12 Attitude toward Bargaining, by Sex and Involvement in Party Politics

	Not Involved in Party Politics					Involved in Party Politics				
	Bargaining					Bargaining				
	N	1	2	3	4	N	1	2	3	4
Female	(15)	53%	40%	7%	0%	(55)	47%	36%	15%	2%
Male	(24)	58%	33%	4%	4%	(68)	21%	37%	31%	12%
	Gamma = .06					Gamma = −.52				

Note: 1 indicates a negative attitude and 4 a positive attitude.

taining their seats—and so it is not surprising that they were also more active in the legislature.

I had expected that elite socialization processes would modify behavioral differences between the sexes, but in fact it accentuated them. Among legislators who had had no involvement in party politics prior to their legislative careers there were no differences between the sexes on either the activity or bargaining scales; however, among legislators who had had some involvement there were differences, men having the relative edge. Particularly with respect to bargaining, the differences between the sexes were quite sharp (table 3.12). A somewhat similar phenomenon occurs when the effects of having held a party office are examined: differences between the sexes were greater among those who had held office than among those who had not, though here sex differences were not markedly sharper in the more active group.* Holding party office is not without effect on women however; women who held office scored higher on the bargaining scale than those who did not. But their "gains" did not keep pace with those of the men. For men the greatest change in behavior comes with involvement in party politics. Men who had had no prior involvement were quite different from those who had had some involvement, whereas for women the changes that occurred took place with office-holding. Involvement in party politics often means little more for women than the carrying out of many routine tasks, a fact which probably explains why prior party involvement itself has little effect on their legislative behavior.

Future political ambitions do indeed affect current legislative behavior,[29] but here again sex differences are accentuated, not modified. Among legislators with no interest in higher office men were somewhat more active than women, while among those with a positive interest the men were considerably more active. Similarly sex differences with respect to bargaining were greater in the ambitious group.† The politically ambitious legislator, knowing that an ability to bargain is almost a prerequisite for successful advancement in American politics, so adapts his current legislative behavior. Women, not being particularly ambitious, need not make such an adaptation. It may be, however, that women are lacking in ambition because, although aware of such requirements, they value their current attitudes over attainment of higher office.

Turning to the effects of seat competition, we see that the method of recruitment is of consequence: there were no sex differences with respect to legislative activity among legislators who had not sought their seat (gamma = −.05), while among those who had sought their seat men were the more active (gamma = −.33). Women who had sought their seat did have a

---

* The gamma increases from −.32 to −.47 for bargaining and from −.17 to −.31 for activity.

† The gamma correlation between sex and activity is −.18 in the no-interest group and −.32 in the interested group; similarly the gamma between sex and bargaining is −.28 in the no-interest group and −.46 in the interested group.

higher level of activity—23 percent of these women scored at the highest activity level, while this was true of only 14 percent of those asked to run—but their level still did not keep pace with that of men. With respect to bargaining, men were somewhat more positively inclined than women among legislators who did not seek their seat (gamma = −.27), but the differences were even greater among those who had sought their seat. (gamma = −.43). The sex differences increase because the method of recruitment is of little consequence for women's attitudes toward bargaining.

A similar pattern emerges upon examination of the consequences of opposition for the nomination. If comparisons are made between those legislators who indicated they faced "very much" opposition and those legislators who faced less opposition, sex differences increase among the former both with respect to activity and bargaining.*

The results that emerge from examining the consequences of change in the composition of a district's population are somewhat difficult to interpret. For the first time, sex differences decrease in the expected direction: in districts with little change the men are the more active, while in districts with considerable change there are no sex differences.† As discussed earlier, the relatively small number of legislators from the "change" districts means that any observed patterns may be factitious. On the other hand this is the only aspect of competition that delimits such a select group, and it may be that only among such a group does the expected modification of sex differences occur. One might feel more confident of this interpretation if sex differences were also modified on the bargaining scale, but in fact the reverse occurs: sex differences are actually accentuated in the "change" districts.‡ This result may again be due only to the

---

* The gamma between sex and activity increases from −.11 to −.40, while between sex and bargaining it increases from −.33 to −.51.

† The gamma between sex and activity is −.31 among legislators from districts with little change and decreases to .08 among legislators from districts with considerable change.

‡ The gamma between sex and bargaining is −.36 in districts with little change and −.74 in districts with considerable change.

small number of cases, or it is possible that the expected modification occurs only with respect to activity. There has been some suggestion with other control variables that bargaining differences are less subject to modification than activity differences. Interpretation is also complicated by the fact that a respondent's evaluation of changes in a district's population is a *very* indirect indicator of seat competition. One can conclude only that there is a suggestion that under intense competition certain behavioral differences between the sexes may be modified.

The goals of this chapter were to document the behavioral differences between female and male legislators and to test the hypothesis that these differences are attenuated by competition. Not surprisingly, the first goal was more readily accomplished than the second. Description is often the easier task. A certain caution must be taken in interpreting these results, for reported sex differences may in certain instances be greater in the actual population. I indicated earlier that the proportion of Democrats among female respondents was less than the proportion of Democrats among female legislators, and that this would affect the results only if sex differences were greater among the Democratic respondents. This in fact was the case on the activity scale, and it is on this scale that reported sex differences are slight.* Democratic women came from lower class-backgrounds than Republican women, a factor which might account for the lower activity of Democratic women.[30] If this difference reflects a real difference between the parties, then the overall sex differences with respect to activity are actually greater in these legislatures.

Our major hypothesis was twofold: the first part, regarding the competitiveness of the recruitment process and political careers, appears to have been partially borne out, while the second part, relating recruitment to legislative behavior, appears, at first glance, not to have been borne out at all. As expected, where

---

* Gamma = −.45 for Democrats and −.16 for Republicans.

seat competition is higher, women who run have more extensive prior involvement in politics (party politics was found to be
the critical involvement). This relationship occurred with respect to each of the indicators of seat competition considered.
One cannot say, however, that similarity to the male pattern is
related in a strict linear fashion to seat competition. When competition is very limited, career patterns may actually be quite
similar, that is, neither sex will have extensive political careers.
Or career patterns may be even more dissimilar in the competitive situation, for women's prior involvements may be greater
than those of men—the case with two of the competition indicators. Women, it would appear, need to compensate for their
"deficiencies" in more competitive situations, a pattern which
was predicted by the model.

But, contrary to expectation, more competitive recruitment
processes accentuate rather than modify behavioral differences
in the legislature itself. The original hypothesis may simply be
incorrect—always a possibility—but an alternative and more
satisfying explanation is that these particular results were due
to the nature of legislative recruitment in these states. Basically
the recruitment process is nonselective, which accounts for the
high proportions of retired persons and women. And though
there is variation among districts, and certainly from state to
state,[31] this variation is limited, for all these states are at the
lower end of the competition spectrum (as measured by relative
availability of legislative seats). My hypothesis, however, dealt
with what would occur under intense competition. On the one
indicator that appeared to delimit the most competitive districts
there was some indication of attenuation.

But the data do suggest some revision of the basic hypothesis.
Perhaps the relationship between competition and sex differences is curvilinear rather than linear. That is, where competition for office is so minimal that recruitment is often a matter
of beseeching volunteers to run, sex differences in terms of
prior careers and legislative behavior are also minimal, simply
because neither sex holds the values of aspiring politicians. At
this level comparisons are being made among concerned citi-

zens rather than among professional politicians. As competition begins to increase, more traditional politicians begin to emerge among males, but competition is still not keen enough to prevent the candidacies of concerned female citizens. Because of these differing types, overall sex differences also begin to emerge here. But at the more intense stages of competition recruitment no longer allows for mere concerned citizens, and this accounts for the drop in women. All candidates must be professional politicians, and consequently sex differences decline. The existence of this hypothesized third stage remains to be tested.

4: Both Woman and Legislator

The role problems of women who have entered the male political stage are the center of this chapter and the next. The major goals here are to delineate these problems and to develop a typology of the roles women play in state legislatures. The notion of human beings as role players is at least as old as Shakespeare's observation, "All the world's a stage." Today the term "role" is so frequently used, both in ordinary discourse and in the social science literature, that one would not ordinarily stop to think about what is meant by the term; but as my usage is not always the same, the variation should be justified at the outset. Overviews of the role-theory literature continually bemoan the lack of consistency in the term's use: "The concept of role remains one of the most overworked and underdeveloped in the social sciences." "Role theory has been beset by conceptual and semantic difficulties." "The concept role is at present still rather vague, nebulous and non-definitive." Shirley Angrist, in an overview of the sex-role literature, comments: "What is meant by sex role? The prime conclusions which emerge from such an inquiry are that sex role is rarely defined, the attempted definitions vary widely, the construct lacks clarity and the three fields [anthropology, psychology, sociology] reveal overlap in usage." [1]

Why not adopt a consistent usage?

The attempt to systematize the role concept in the social sciences was begun in the 1930s by the social psychologist George Herbert Mead and the anthropologist Ralph Linton.[2] The major theoretical expositions in sociology appeared in the 1950s with the writings of Talcott Parsons and Robert K. Merton.[3] Role was a central element in these theorists' conceptual schemes of the structure and functioning of social systems and the dynamics of individual behavior. Political science has essentially borrowed the concept from these other disciplines, the most thoroughgoing and self-conscious use of the concept occurring in Wahlke, Eulau, Buchanan, and Ferguson's *The Legislative System* (1962). These authors, comparing four state legislatures, used the role concept to link the behavior of individual legislators to the problem of legislative structure and function. Role, for any individual legislator, refers "to a coherent set of 'norms' of behavior which are thought by those involved in the interactions being viewed to apply to all persons who occupy the position of legislator." Emphasis is on the relationship for the individual legislator between expressed norms and behavior: "The concept postulates that individual legislators are aware of the norms constituting the role and consciously adapt their behavior to them in some fashion." [4] Their conception essentially excludes personality factors, paying no attention to the extent to which role definition and performance are in part a response to personality needs. [5]

The other major work that is important for a discussion of the roles of state legislators is James Barber's study of the Connecticut legislature, *The Lawmakers*. [6] Barber, in contrast to Wahlke and company, does not develop his concept of role at great length, but he does concern himself with the needs of the self and demonstrates how different personality needs generate different patterns of adjustment to legislative life. Both *The Legislative System* and *The Lawmakers* deal with the functional consequences for the legislative institution of the roles held by individual actors. *The Legislative System* is a formal attempt to use the role concept in a precise fashion, while *The Lawmakers* employs role theory more informally. Both, however, suffer from what Daniel J. Levinson has described as the "unitary" conception of the social role. They merge the three aspects of role— structurally given demands, member's orientation or conception of part, and actions—and thereby assume a "close fit between behavior and disposition (attitude, value), between societal prescription and individual adaptation." [7] This may be an "unrealistic and theoretically constricting" conception, as Levinson calls it. However when, as in the present study, the available data do not permit systematic empirical investigation of the three aspects, the rigorous analytical distinctions that are desirable cannot always be drawn. This may lead to a certain looseness and inconsistency in usage.[8] An additional problem is that the concept of "sex role" is rarely defined in the literature and has been primarily investigated in the family setting. There is little foundation on which to build when studying sex roles in institutional settings not directly related to the family. The varied approaches to the general concept of role in sociology and political science do, however, generate several questions relevant to the study of sex roles.

There are four principal questions to which we will now turn. First: *What are the general problems facing persons who simultaneously occupy the status of woman and the status of state legislator?* The focus here is on the norms, expectations, taboos, responsibilities, and opportunities associated with individuals located in a system of social and political relationships. Role theorists use the terms "status" and "position" interchangeably to indicate the general idea of social location. I have chosen the term "status" because it "connotes the idea of differential rankings among a set of persons or social locations," and I am assuming that many of the problems discovered derive from the fact that the individuals being examined occupy "social locations" which are differentially ranked by the society at large.[9] I emphasize the notion of "problem" because I am not only interested in describing the situations of individuals who hold such statuses, but also committed ultimately to solutions. I assume here that such individuals face certain conflicts or strains, that these conflicts are the reason for the infrequent "entrance" of women on to the political stage, and that it is necessary to understand the exact nature of such conflicts in order to remedy the basic situation. The infrequent assumption of political leadership roles by women is a problem for a democratic society.

The second question explores personal role definitions: *How do individual women legislators orient themselves to the parts they play in the legislature?* The focus here is on adaptation to the legislative environment. I assume that the individual's role definition or conception is not only a response to the structural demands of the legislative institution and the individual family situation but is also influenced by aspects of the individual's personality—basic values, life goals, and conception of self or "ego identity." It is expected that there will be some variation in individual role conceptions, and that it will be possible to identify modal types. I will also be concerned with the relationship between role conceptions and role performance or behavior, and the implications of certain types of behavior for the overall status of women in society.

The third question concerns the functional significance of the tasks or acts performed by women legislators: *What functions do women serve in state legislatures?* The focus here will be on the overall significance of the tasks performed by women as they relate to the maintenance of the legislature as a policy making institution, and the extent to which these functions vary in different legislative environments.

The social-psychological perspective of the first question (problems facing individuals who are both women and legislators) focuses on the implications *for individuals* of conflicting role expectations. But one can also consider the implications of such conflict for the institution. Such a perspective leads to yet another question concerning sex roles: *What are the political and social consequences of allowing individuals to occupy both the status of woman and the status of state legislator?*

I said earlier that one of the problems with much of the work on sex roles is that it concentrates almost exclusively on the family setting. The present research suffers from a related problem, the tendency to focus almost exclusively on women's sex roles—"the implication being that it has only to do with women." [10] There is no assumption here that sex roles are unique to women. I have concentrated on women for two unrelated reasons which dovetailed conveniently for this inquiry: (1) limitations of time, and (2) the peculiar situation of women in contemporary society. Limitations of time made it impossible to conduct a large number of personal interviews; interviews with both sexes would have been necessary to deal more directly with the central theoretical interest of this research—the theory that the exigencies of modern culture dictate movement away from the differentiation of sex roles and toward "androgynous" life-styles. The sociologist Michael Banton believes that role differentiation—"the extent to which incumbency of one role is independent of incumbency of other roles—is related to the technological and productive complexity of societies." "As societies advance in productive and technological sophistication the behavioral relevance of age and sex roles is restricted and declines in importance." Without interviews with both sexes in varying social and political situations I can deal with this concern only in a very tentative fashion. But as Banton notes, "a category like sex roles is not a homogeneous one: the role of female tends to be less independent of other roles than that of the male." [11] Simone de Beauvoir, in *The Second Sex* (1952), describes the same phenomenon in somewhat different terminology:

> What is a woman? To state the question is, to me, to suggest, at once, a preliminary answer. The fact that I ask it is in itself significant. A man never gets the notion of writing a book on the peculiar situation of the human male. A man never begins by presenting himself as an individual of a certain sex; it goes without saying that he is a man. The terms masculine and feminine are used symmetrically only as a matter of form, as on legal papers. In actuality the relation of the two sexes is not quite like that of two electrical poles, for man represents both the positive and the neutral, as is indicated by the common use of man to designate human beings in general.[12]

Since the study of political behavior among political elites has been essentially the study of male behavior, there is still much to be learned on the subject of sex roles and political roles by concentrating exclusively on the "peculiar" situation of women.

Matters of Method

My data for the exploration of sex roles were derived from personal interviews with women legislators serving in the 1972 legislative session. Ten legislators were interviewed in Connecticut and twelve in New Hampshire. The interviews were all conducted in the Capitol buildings of each state.

The interview was based on a series of open-ended questions which gave respondents considerable opportunity to introduce information they felt to be relevant and to express their feelings and reactions. (See appendix 6 for the interview schedule.) I began with general questions about particular topics and then probed further into particular choices, feelings, and reactions. This provided the opportunity for the respondents to initiate discussion of responsibilities, advantages, or restrictions that flowed from the fact that they were women. In cases where the respondent did not take advantage of such opportunities I probed for the presence of such considerations. This seemed to be the most unbiased method of ascertaining the salience of sex roles to individual respondents.

Because the purpose of the study was not only to explore the role concepts and problems of individual women legislators but also to examine the role of women in legislative institutions, the selection of research sites was necessarily limited to those few states with a sufficient number of female legislators to permit systematic study. Examination of more than one state was considered essential for the purpose of comparison. In view of the increasing urbanization of the nation and the particular interest here in the effects of urbanization on sex-role differentiation, Connecticut and New Hampshire were appropriate research sites, being the only states (of the possible four) with sizable urban centers. The two states differ with respect to such matters as the competition-for-seats ratio, size of the lower house, intensity of legislative operations, salaries and staff for members, and character of the party system in the legislature. Therefore it should be possible to relate the role of women to structural differences of legislatures.

These data suffer from the inevitable bias of willingness to cooperate. (See appendix 5 for further details on the selection of interview subjects.) The interviews themselves were conducted in an exploratory fashion, which means they were not all precisely alike. Given the close scheduling of the interview sessions there was little opportunity actually to observe the legislators as they acted out their roles and interacted with other legislators, constituents, and lobbyists. Considering these data limitations and the exploratory nature of the project, the results presented here should be treated as working hypotheses in need of further testing and refinement.

Some of the generalizations presented in these chapters are supported by a set of interviews with four female state legislators conducted by another researcher in New York State during the 1973 legislative session. The interview schedule was an adaptation of the schedule used in Connecticut and New Hampshire. The interviews were all tape-recorded in the legislators' offices, and the data were made available to me in the form of verbatim transcripts.

Before dealing with the results of the interviews it is necessary to draw a dimensional portrait of the women legislators, for the responses are obviously conditioned by their background characteristics. Although these interviews are representative of women serving in Connecticut and New Hampshire, the question might be raised as to how representative they are of women legislators in other states. Since I am interested in making some generalizations that might be applicable beyond Connecticut and New Hampshire, note should be taken if these women do differ considerably from their counterparts in the rest of the nation. (See appendix 1 for a dimensional portrait of women state legislators in the nation.)

In Connecticut all the women legislators had been married. At the time of the interviews one was divorced and one was widowed. All of the women had children, and most of their families were small. Their children were generally adults: only one woman had a child under eighteen years of age (sixteen). The legislators' median age bracket was fifty-five to fifty-nine, and as table 4.1 indicates their level of education varied considerably. Most of them listed their occupation as "housewife," and half had *family* incomes of more than $20,000 annually.

Table 4.1 Social Background Characteristics of Legislators Interviewed

	Connecticut	New Hampshire
Number of children		
1	3	1
2	4	3
3	1	3
4	2	3
5	0	1
	(N = 10)	(N = 11)
Age		
21–29	0	1
30–39	0	2
40–49	1	2
50–59	5	6
60–69	2	1
70 or over	1	0
	(N = 9)	(N = 12)
Family Income ($)		
5,000–9,999	1	3
10,000–14,999	2	5
15,000–19,999	1	1
20,000–24,999	2	1
25,000 or over	3	1
	(N = 9)	(N = 11)
Marital Status		
Single	8	1
Divorced	1	1
Married	1	10
	(N = 10)	(N = 12)
Education		
High School	3	4
Some college	2	2
College	2	6
M.A.	3	0
	(N = 10)	(N = 12)
Occupation		
Teacher	—	1
Nurse	—	1
Pharmacist's assistant	—	1
Social worker	—	1
Bartender	—	1
Field worker for U.S. senator	—	1
Housewife	7	6
None	1	—
Full-time legislator	1	—
	(N = 9)	(N = 12)

Note: Totals vary because some interviewees omitted some information on their questionnaires.

In New Hampshire all but one of the women legislators had been married and most had families, but here family size was considerably greater than in Connecticut. Five of the women had children under eighteen years of age, and two had children under ten years. The ages of these legislators varied considerably and many were college educated. Half of the women had occupations other than housewife; the typical family income was between $10,000 and $15,000 annually.

In terms of socioeconomic background these New England women were fairly representative of women legislators in general, but they were somewhat less educated then their counterparts outside New England. During this session there were no women lawyers in either legislature, and hence there was no opportunity to investigate firsthand the consequences of legal training for the female legislator's political career or mode of adaptation to the legislative environment. Fortunately, however, the interviewees in New York were all female lawyer-legislators.

Before they assumed legislative office, the political careers of most of the women in Connecticut and New Hampshire had been limited. Most had some kind of prior community or political involvement. In each state there were only two women who had not held any party or public office; the rest had, but usually only one or two local posts such as school board member, city clerk, or ballot inspector. In each state there were only three women who had held four or more different local offices prior to their legislative careers. Their length of tenure in the legislature varied considerably. In Connecticut the number of terms served ranged from one to twelve, in New Hampshire from one to four.

Hypotheses

The first consideration is the role problems facing persons who simultaneously occupy the status of female and state legislator. I am interested in describing the situation faced by such women, but I also want to test some general propositions about role strain and role-strain resolution. Role strain or role conflict is frequently dealt with in the role-theory literature.[13] The notion that most individuals routinely experience role strain has been developed by William Goode.

All individuals take part in many different role relationships, for each of which there will be somewhat different obligations. Among these there may be either contradictory performances required . . . or conflicts of time, place, or resources. . . . The individual is thus likely to face a wide, distracting, and sometimes conflicting array of obligations. . . . Role strain—difficulty in meeting given role demands—is therefore *normal*. In general the individual's total role obligations are over-demanding.[14]

William C. Mitchell views the American elective public official as subject to considerable strain stemming from a variety of sources.[15] Role strain is certainly not unique to women legislators. Women legislators share with their male colleagues the strain that results from "the conflicts originating within or among the various roles that constitute an elective public office." These strains—between representing one's district and being a member of a particular political party, for example—are something to which incumbents of the legislative role will be subject because they "are patterned along the structure of the roles or norms that make up the system." But not all incumbents will respond in the same way. Although we cannot directly test whether female incumbents react to such strains differently from male incumbents, we can observe how the women respond. "Responding," however, is not necessarily a conscious activity: "self-awareness of a role strain is not a criterion of its existence."[16] It is even possible that women exhibit immunity to strains that cause considerable anxiety among men.

A legislator of either sex experiences the role strain that results from what Mitchell terms "private versus public roles." "Behavior which is regarded as acceptable or even admirable in private life may not be so regarded in public office."[17] Every legislator simultaneously holds other roles which may make demands on performance, time, or resources which conflict with the demands of the legislative role. Any legislator may have held certain previous roles involving behavioral norms that make adaptation to the legislature somewhat difficult. Although all legislators are subject to the conflict between private and public roles, they are not all subject to such strains to the same degree. If sex roles are considered in the category of "private roles," then female legislators should generally be subject to considerably more private-versus-public role strain than male legislators. The feminine role is associated with certain behavioral expectations which in many respects are antithetical to the expectations of the legislative role. In addition, the female legislator may be wife, mother, and homemaker, roles which normally are very demanding on time and resources.

There are specific behavioral expectations associated with the sex role of woman which make that role incongruent with the role of legislator. Cynthia Fuchs Epstein writes:

> All societies define sex roles according to their images of the ideal man or woman. It cannot be too radical to assert that no human being is unaffected by these definitions, or can escape being measured according to these cultural images. Although preferred female attributes and behavior vary over a considerable range, in most societies there is a core of preferred and imputed female attributes. In American society these include, among others, personal warmth and empathy, sensitivity and emotionalism, grace, charm, compliance, dependence, and deference. . . . The image of woman includes as well some non-characteristics: lack of aggressiveness, lack of personal involvement and egotism, lack of persistence (unless it be for the benefit of a family member), and lack of ambitious drive.

Epstein is concerned with the consequences of such images for the woman who is interested in a professional career.

> Conflict faces the would-be career woman, for the core of attributes found in most professional and occupational roles is considered to be masculine: persistence and drive, personal dedication, aggressiveness, emotional detachment,

and a kind of sexless matter-of-factness equated with intellectual performance.[18]

These behavioral attributes certainly are part of the idealized image of any public officeholder, and so the woman entering the political world is likely to face many of the same strains that beset the woman professional.

However, certain other norms pervade the world of politics—particularly the legislative arena—which increase the degree of strain. The role requirements for the legislator (as opposed to those for a judge) demand skill at negotiation and compromise, an attribute which is not part of the idealized image of the feminine role.[19] Negotiating is a part of the idealized image of the legislative role held by legislators themselves, but in society at large there is an implicit, if not explicit, belief that negotiating is but a euphemism for shady dealing.[20] The image of politics as something dirty, where the real action takes place in smoke-filled backrooms and bars, is a prominent theme in the American political culture. But in the cult of True Womanhood women are given the solemn responsibility of upholding the pillars of civilization and the Republic. The preservation of a woman's virtues—piety, purity, submissiveness, and domesticity—is therefore crucial not only to the femininity of any individual woman but to the very maintenance of society; hence women must be shielded from anything dirty or impure.[21] The woman legislator is likely to be subject to considerable role strain due to the conflict in images between the ideal woman and the ideal legislator.

The woman legislator is also subject to strains stemming from the other roles she is likely to hold—wife, mother, and housekeeper. The male legislator may also be husband, father, and breadwinner—which in some cases can cause considerable conflict. But, like the male professional, he is somewhat protected

by the existence in his environment of a hierarchy of values which preclude, for the most part, the necessity of conscious decision. Unless family needs reach crisis proportions, the demands of his work come first. And neither he

nor his wife is faced with the problem of choice in a condition of crisis.[22]

Epstein sees the woman professional as subject to considerable
role strain because she does not have the benefit of unam-
biguous norms in apportioning her time and resources between
two major responsibilities. The woman legislator is likely to be
subject to this same strain and to additional conflicts that flow
from her position as a public elected official. Whereas the professional woman can resolve her role problems privately, the
woman legislator must justify her individual solution publicly.[23]
The fate of the female politician's family is often a matter of
public concern.[24]

I have been detailing those norms of the social structure
which, given the woman legislator's location in that structure,
are likely to subject her to considerable strain. Not all role incumbents, however, consciously experience the predicted
strains. Suggesting that there are certain cultural contradictions
to which female legislators may be subject is not to say that a
particular individual will necessarily be aware of incompatible
expectations.[25] Role-conflict resolution is possible only in situations where the individual perceives contradictory expectations
and feels compelled to choose among alternatives. The question
arises whether it is possible to predict the type of woman legislator who will perceive these contradictory expectations. Sex is an
important criterion for the allocation of roles in all societies. "A
person's sex role usually affects the way people respond to him
or her more than does any other role." [26] Sex roles are so basic
because sex-role socialization begins in the early years of life in
the most intimate of primary groups, the family, and is reinforced continually in all groups and institutions throughout the
years when an individual is developing a sense of self. In indus-
trial societies individual achievement or merit is also a criterion
for the allocation of roles, the importance of this criterion being
stressed primarily in the schools and other "public" institutions.
The values of equality and achievement are decidedly explicit in
the American ideology; sex-role differentiation, on the other

hand, while not an explicit part of the ideology, does heavily in-fluence practices. Observers have noted that sex-role ideologies tend to be considerably more egalitarian than practices in indus-trial societies, while in traditional societies the reverse is true.[27] As a consequence of these discrepancies, individuals in modern industrial societies are generally unaware of the extent to which sex roles condition their behavior. One of the primary issues raised by the contemporary women's movement is the power of the unconscious ideology of sexism.[28]

If sex roles are such a basic determinant of role relationships, while at the same time their influence is largely unnoticed, cer-tain predictions can be made as to the type of woman legislator who will perceive the contradictory behaviors required by sex-role norms and legislative norms. The legislator's awareness of the salience of sex roles would appear to be crucial. Therefore:

> 1. The greater the legislator's consciousness of the salience of sex roles, the greater the likelihood that the legislator will experience role conflict between traditional feminine role ex-pectations and professional expectations.

Consciousness of the salience of sex roles will also be related to role-conflict resolution:

> 2. Among legislators who perceive sex roles as highly salient, role-conflict resolution will favor the professional role; among legislators who perceive sex roles as nonsalient, role-conflict resolution will favor the traditional feminine role.

Role-conflict resolution favors the professional role among legislators who perceive sex roles as highly salient because such women are likely to feel frustrated with the limitations of the traditional feminine role. Harriet Holter observes: "To feel frus-trated with one's sex role one must consider it legitimate to compare it with that of the opposite sex. Only if two categories are regarded as similar in some way is it meaningful to compare them." [29] An individual who believes that intrinsic differences between the sexes preclude comparisons is unlikely to feel frus-trated with the traditional feminine role, and so in any situation where conflicting expectations are perceived will invariably choose the feminine role.

What are the general problems facing persons who simultaneously occupy the status of female and the status of state legislator? The interview material describes the actual situation of such women as they perceive it and provides a basis for judging the relevance of the two propositions concerning role conflict. But before considering this dual status a preliminary question is in order.

How does holding the status of female affect an individual's opportunity even to acquire the status of state legislator? Clearly the basic cultural condition discussed earlier, that politics is defined as a masculine endeavor and that women are generally socialized to select themselves out of active political involvement, is the primary factor limiting a woman's opportunity to acquire any political office. Many of the legislators, when asked what they thought to be the major problems women have had to face in politics, said, "themselves." However, the concern here is not with general cultural conditions, but with the specific factors which operate either to a woman's advantage or to her disadvantage in obtaining political office. The "peculiar" conditions faced by female candidates in New Hampshire and Connecticut warrant mention at this point.

As chapter 2 demonstrated, historically the structural conditions in Connecticut and New Hampshire were favorable to the election of women, and in New Hampshire the conditions still obtain. The relative availability of legislative seats (large chambers for small populations) created a situation in which there was minimal competition for seats, thus enabling women to be elected. Over the years women have been elected to these legislatures in sufficiently large numbers that the status of female is only moderately "deviant," and consequently whatever advantages or disadvantages usually accrue to a woman simply because of her sex probably do not occur with the same frequency or intensity in these states.

In the introduction to her biographical study of women in

public life, *Few Are Chosen*, Peggy Lamson writes, "For the vast majority of women now in public office at all levels, winning the election has been far easier than capturing the nomination." [30] But as the model developed here would predict, gaining the nomination generally is not a problem for women in New Hampshire. The following response from a New Hampshire legislator captures the flavor of a common sort of occurrence in that state:

> And we had filled the slate in Ward 2 . . . this is the ward that I live in, and we had this man who was going to run. The position was open—I have forgotten how come. Two days before the filing date he informed us that he wasn't going to be able to run after all—so frantically another lady and I between us called fifty people, and we simply could not find anyone. You know the *pay isn't that great* in the state of New Hampshire, and you simply can't take the time off. So I said, gee, *if nobody else will, I'll go.* So two minutes before the filing deadline I went down and signed on.

This pervasive problem of recruiting suitable candidates does not mean that a woman can have the nomination for the asking in all districts. Several legislators mentioned that in certain towns women were "not encouraged." One legislator recalled that after she won the primary the "father" of her town greeted her with, "I didn't know ——— was ready for a woman yet." These "pockets of resistance" indicate the strength of underlying norms. Attitudes about proper sex roles can remain rigid even when political expediency suggests that they be modified.

In Connecticut most of the women in the house reported little trouble in securing their nominations, but there were no reports of desperate searches for candidates. Some of the women did say that they felt that getting the nomination was the major problem women have had to face in politics:

> I think there is strong resistance on the part of political committees to seeking out women or in many cases to giving them an even deal with male candidates.

Q: *Do you attribute any of your problems in securing the nomination to your being a woman?*
A: I think there is a little problem there. I think our local town chairman—much as I admire him, he is a very capable politician—I feel some of the women agree with me, he had a little difficulty accepting women, probably finds them a little hard to work with.

It has been noted elsewhere that party leaders are generally more likely to be receptive to the nomination of women when their party's chance of victory is remote. India Edwards, for many years vice-chairman of the Democratic National Committee, has commented, "If the party backs a woman you can be pretty sure they do it because they think it's a lost cause but they know they have to have some candidate." [31] One legislator in Connecticut described her nomination as follows:

Well, it was a very funny thing. I come from a district which hadn't had a Democrat in office since the Civil War, roughly. And none of us took campaigning seriously, including me. . . . So the nomination as always was open.

It would appear that in situations where legislative seats are desirable a woman will receive the nomination under one of two conditions—either when the party thinks the cause is hopeless or when the woman wins the nomination in a primary fight. A Democratic senator from a completely Republican area in New Hampshire, swept into office during the 1964 Johnson landslide, remarks: "It was fun to run because you didn't think you were going to win. We had a real good time that election." A legislator in Connecticut observes:

I've had two primary contests . . . they really don't like me being in there, in the legislative job, because they can't control me. . . . They don't like women in power, many of them. These small-town political chairmen, small-town bosses—they like a man, and they like a man they can sit in the back room with and decide these things, and of course I didn't qualify either way.

A senator from New York who began her political career by winning in a district her party had written off summarized the situation of women legislators like this:

> I think one of the interesting things I've seen . . . I've become active in the National Order of Women Legislators, which is an organization of other women state legislators, and I find that my situation is very similar to an overwhelming number of women who were elected to state legislative positions. We either won primaries in our parties or we were nominated by men who controlled political parties in districts which were so overwhelmingly of the opposite party that they were kind of hopeless districts, and therefore they had reached the understanding among themselves that *these were not districts they could win anyway so what's the difference if we let a woman try.*

What is the situation faced by the female candidate, having received the nomination, in trying to win the seat? Generalizing about campaign experiences for the New Hampshire house presents certain difficulties because of the situation described as follows by a legislator:

> I'm afraid there wasn't any campaign. You see, this job up here doesn't pay you anything. It is ridiculous. So all I did mainly was file. We did have a candidates' night, and people knew how I stood on taxes because I had worked for a candidate who stood for a broad-based tax.

Campaigning, if it exists at all, is minimal in these small New Hampshire districts, where generally the women candidates are already well known in their wards through their local party or community work. In Connecticut, where the legislators could at least reflect on their campaign experiences, being a woman was generally viewed as an advantage in door-to-door campaigning:

> Yes, I love to meet people, and I like to go into their homes and sit and talk with them. . . .

Q: *Have you ever felt that you were received more warmly because you were a woman?*
A: Yes, I think so.

Q: *Why do you think this is so?*
A: Well, I think when you go up and say "I'm so-and-so," and you say, "I'm campaigning for the legislature and I would like to talk to you; do you have any problems?; Do you have something you want to tell me about," they like it. I think people are much more standoffish if a man comes along.

I did a tremendous amount of door-to-door campaigning. I got so terribly caught up in my own darn campaign that it kind of snowballed—that's what happened to me. In fact it was the first door-to-door campaign the town had ever seen. I may have had a slight advantage because when you knock on the door during the day, women will . . . I never feared that they wouldn't talk to me, but you know if a man came you might not necessarily stand there and talk about things, and I had a lot of satisfying personal conversations—really very, very productive and a tremendous educational experience for me. . . . And possibly being a woman helped a little bit.

The ideal image of the woman as the empathetic being who deals with personal problems can be an advantage in face-to-face encounters. In addition, a strange woman at the door is not very likely to be perceived as a physical threat. Women generally can benefit from certain traditional behavioral expectations about women's aptitudes, and sometimes they can use the resources provided by the traditional female-associated roles. Several of the housewives mentioned that campaigning was easier for them because they "had time" or "were available." The public's perception of these other roles can sometimes be very important. Who the candidate's husband is and his position in the community can be of consequence:

A factor that helped me was my name. My husband is from a prominent family and is active in the Catholic Church.

> My husband is a _____, and the _____'s have lived in
> _____ for a good many years.

> I had an advantage because my husband is a physician in a
> professional town, and people probably figured he was a
> smart, able doctor and therefore smart enough to marry a
> smart, able wife.

or,

> Before they got through they weren't so happy they had
> given me the nomination, because my husband is president
> of the foundry and in the steel business, and they had a big
> strike. And they [the opposition] used the management-
> versus-labor thing on me, and that was kind of unpleasant.
> I didn't mind it as much as my party did, because they
> thought I was going to lose. I almost did.

It was suggested earlier that any woman in an elective public
office would face certain strains because of pressure to justify
publicly her handling of family responsibilities. None of the
legislators in Connecticut or New Hampshire mentioned such
problems, perhaps because very few of them had young families
and because women candidates for the legislature are not un-
common in these states. However, a woman legislator in New
York reports:

> One of my biggest problems was with the young mothers
> who had young children, and because I had young children
> they'd say: "Well, how can you do it?" This was because a
> new baby is almost a full-time job—it *is* a full-time job. So,
> I would simply arrange to have a little coffee or tea at my
> own home and show them how I did it. It was quite appar-
> ent to them: I have a lovely home, and I have a lot of house-
> hold help, and there was no problem. This seemed to take
> care of that issue, which was probably the place I hit at the
> most as far as problems.

Delegation of tasks has been suggested as one technique of
reducing role strain.[32] A woman legislator can delegate some of

her family responsibilities; but she must be extremely careful in
how she handles the situation, because, as Epstein notes:

> It is not even as onerous to be labelled a poor father as it is
> to be called a poor mother. . . . Professors who prefer their
> work to their wives or children are usually "understood" or
> "forgiven" . . . the lady professional who gives any indica-
> tion of being more absorbed in work than in her husband or
> family is neither understood nor forgiven. The woman, un-
> like the man, cannot spend "too much time" with her fam-
> ily.[33]

Advantages or disadvantages may stem simply from the rarity of
a woman candidate. The only legislator in either New Hampshire or Connecticut to refer to this factor was a Connecticut
senator, a species much rarer than assemblywomen in Connecticut.

> Q: *Are there any particular advantages during a cam-
> paign in being a woman?*
> A: No, I don't think so, except that people look on you
> perhaps with a little more interest perhaps than just an-
> other man, because we aren't so common in numbers.

In New York a woman candidate for either the assembly or
the senate is something of a novelty:

> You're different if you're a woman running for office today.
> There's no question about it. I think to some extent perhaps
> you get—well, I'm not sure it happened before the election,
> but it certainly happened after the election—you tend to get
> a little better press coverage. . . . If you were sitting up
> there on a whole stage of candidates and there's one
> woman and twelve men, people may go away thinking,
> "There's a woman running for office."

> I got a tremendously good treatment from the press. This
> was because they hadn't been exposed to a real campaign
> in this district for a long time, and I think the novelty of a
> woman gave me a little more exposure. I found myself hav-

ing a double advantage because I wound up on the news pages as hard news but also in feature articles written about me in the woman's pages. So it turned out to be an advantage. Practically every women's editor in the area did an article on my campaign. So I got some extra coverage that way, which sometimes actually produced for me volunteers, because women who would read the women's pages would call up the headquarters and ask, could they help?

The ability of women candidates to attract women volunteers was noted by another assemblywoman in New York:

Q: *Do you believe that you were ever helped by being a woman in your campaign?*
A: Oh, yes. Getting all those women volunteers. Many of them did it just, I'm sure, because they wanted to see a woman get it. Even though this was well before the popular notion of the women's second wave of liberation. Much to my surprise, a group of women that I thought would not support me turned out to be very supportive, were the older women who had been active in the original suffrage movement. And the fact that they're sort of the dowagers and very respected in the community and identified primarily with the most conservative things in the world made me think that this group would not be with me, but I was very surprised to discover that they were very helpful.

Part of sex-role training in this society is that women are *supposed* to be treated with extra courtesy because of their "pedestal" position. These norms affect the way many people will respond to a woman's campaign, and although it is difficult to assess whether the assorted rituals have any real impact on the outcome of a campaign, they do affect the style of interaction between the candidate and the public.

If you're standing in a subway station at 7 in the morning and somebody comes barreling to get the subway train and you stick out your hand to say "hello," just because of society and the way we've been programmed they might be somewhat reluctant to sock you in the face than if you're a man. They might be somewhat taken aback for a second and friendlier after.

Running some years ago I was still in the area in which people were pleased to have a woman come in and I think given certain considerations because she was a woman . . . into a speaking engagement or into a meeting to talk or even door-to-door campaigning. People were extremely courteous and polite.

Running for office also involves money. Given the nature of the legislator's job in New Hampshire, campaign expenses for seeking a seat in the lower house often involve little more than paying the filing fee. In Connecticut it appeared that most of the women in the lower house spent at least a small amount of money on their campaigns. There was only one woman who felt that she received less money because of her sex, an older woman who repeatedly averred that since reapportionment, with all the young men running, things were getting difficult for women. A New Hampshire senator felt that the only problem she had as a woman in campaigning was money:

> I hate to ask for money. It's very difficult for a woman to go out and ask for money for herself. I can go out and ask for money for men—I don't mind hitting someone and saying "can you help?"—but I just don't have it in me to do it for myself, and I think men are reluctant to go out and ask for money for women.
> Q: *Why?*
> A: I don't know. I've never had a man say, "let me go out and get money for you."

This point was pursued with a woman senator in Connecticut, but this senator felt that people were more than willing to contribute to a female candidate, especially if she is the "victim of political machinations." However, she felt no reluctance to actively solicit money for her cause. The data do not allow for any generalizations about the effect of female status on a candidate's ability to obtain campaign funds.

The interviews suggest that the primary obstacle for a woman candidate is the nomination. There is little evidence of a generally hostile public. The only legislator who seemed to feel that men had all the advantages in the campaign was one elderly woman in Connecticut who was not sure of herself:

> A couple of us had very nice treatment, but I do think that the men seem to have the advantage, and there are a great many people who think that men can do a better job.

Individual women suggested particular problems which they felt only women candidates faced:

> I don't think the obstacles are any different. A woman has to present herself to the public the same way. Well, maybe not. Sometimes if there's the least little bit of suspicion around a woman, other women will probably crucify her.

One legislator in New Hampshire felt that women candidates were not taken seriously, but when other legislators were probed on this point they did not concur. Although there is always that segment of the public that will not vote for a woman, simply because she is a woman (a New York legislator was the only one to express this sentiment), there is also that segment that will vote for a woman candidate because she is a woman.[34] I am referring here not to politicized persons who will vote for a woman out of a set of ideological convicions about rectifying past wrongs (although this segment is very likely growing), but rather to those persons who simply "like a woman candidate because they know she'll be there." In states like Connecticut and New Hampshire, where the family breadwinner has no choice but to supplement his legislative salary through outside endeavors, women are simply "good cheap labor."[35] Although the available data do not permit a direct test of the extent to which the public is influenced by such considerations, many of the women legislators felt that their candidacies were helped because people appreciated that women did not have the conflict of outside jobs.

How does holding the status of female affect the individual's interactions in the legislative arena? I shall examine how these interactions are affected, first by the behavioral expectations associated with the feminine role and then by the other roles the female legislator is likely to hold. The concern in both areas is with resultant pressures and opportunities.

The female legislator's interactions with her constituents, lobbyists, and colleagues are initially mediated, and sometimes continually mediated, by certain images or conventionally held stereotypes about women. I discussed earlier certain ideal images concerning women. These are part of the conventional culture, and I have already shown how they influence the campaign experience. But the conventional culture also indicates its valuation of women by a series of unflattering stereotypic images: women are overly talkative, overly emotional, illogical, sneaky, gossipy, indecisive, and vain. Many of the female legislators, particularly those concerned with being effective and respected as legislators, find themselves continually fighting a rearguard action against the specter of these stereotypes.

Constituents

The female legislator is perceived as being ever available by her constituents. This can be viewed as a negative pressure, particularly when constituents insist on telephoning in the middle of the night, or as a positive opportunity enabling the legislator to solidify relationships with constituents, thereby enhancing reelection prospects. There seemed to be some disagreement as to whether it was only women constituents, or all constituents, who were prone to contact with female legislators, but there was a definite consensus among the women (admittedly I do not know what the consensus would be among men) that women legislators received considerably more calls than their male colleagues.

If a woman has a problem at home, she calls me. They think time means nothing if you're a woman. They think you're available—come in with problems that have nothing to do with the senate. *A woman would think twice about calling a man about personal problems.*

I think constituents are more apt to call a woman.
Q: *Why do you think this is so?*
A: Because I have had about one thousand more phone calls than my predecessor, who was a man. He tried to meet the response by holding office hours, and he gave it up because he never had any phone calls. And I hold office hours regularly every Saturday morning in the town hall, and I often have a line waiting outside my door.
Q: *Why do you think this is so?*
A: I think it is because *they feel they can talk to a woman.*
Q: *Is it mostly women?*
A: No, it's mostly men.

Well, I think the demands on the women from the constituents are on the *personal issues* more. There may be a feeling of contact with a representative because she is a woman, on a personal issue, more than there would be if it were a male.

I have had more people ask me questions about what goes on and how things happen than asked my husband [who was her predecessor]. And the only thing I can think of is because I have been a housewife and involved in things and they know me maybe a little better they feel they can ask me questions. And I'm not going to say it is stupid, *or make them feel that they are stupid*—not that my husband would either, but I think they feel a little more at ease to ask me something.

A woman legislator in New Hampshire was particularly concerned with how relationships with constituents might be affected if the size of the assembly were reduced:

Well, as it happens, I am not in favor of reducing the size of the house. For the simple reason that people call me who would never bother to call—that *they would be afraid to call someone else who was in a higher class of people.* I am simply an ordinary housewife, and I have housewives call me. . . . I don't think you would get this close to the grass roots if you had a lawyer—a high-paid salary man—these people would be afraid to approach somebody like a lawyer or something along this line.

Constituents may feel more comfortable in approaching a female representative because of certain feelings about women's aptitudes and inclinations. They might rationalize along these lines: "Since women like to talk, they won't mind if I just talk." But the response of the "ordinary housewife" in New Hampshire suggests that the process may be a bit more complex. Sidney Verba has hypothesized that the average citizen is not comfortable elevating others to positions of authority, because the very act of choosing someone to govern implies an inequality between the citizen and the leader. However, if political leaders also possess some other attribute which is highly valued in society—for example, wealth or education—then the exercise of their power is less challenging to the persons who elect them.[36] This psychological explanation would account for the reluctance of both men and women to put women in positions of authority. But feeling more comfortable about choosing a person of higher status in the isolation of the voting booth is one thing; actually approaching such a person about one's personal problems is very different. Emphasis on inequality between the voter and the leader may make leadership selection less threatening, but interactions with unfamiliar persons are likely to be less threatening if inequalities of status are de-emphasized. Status anxieties may partially account for the reluctance to elevate women to positions of political authority; but once leaders have been selected, interactions between constituents and women leaders are likely to provoke less status anxiety than comparable interactions with male leaders. In addition, the objective perception that a woman is in the position of authority very likely leads to the subjective evaluation that the office itself is not very awesome.

Colleagues

The expectation that women's special aptitudes lie in the area of personal relations also govern the female legislator's initial encounters in the legislature itself. Women are presumed to be more interested in issue areas that deal with "people" rather than with "things"—health, education, welfare, juveniles, and corrections, as opposed to fiscal policy and administrative and legal matters. Generally this expectation on the part of the male leadership involved in assigning legislators to committees does not present female legislators with an unwelcome obligation, for generally the expectations prove correct: most of the women *are interested* in these issues. Not a single legislator expressed any unhappiness about her initial committee assignments: comments such as "I was pleased"—"delighted"—"thrilled" were typical. Several of the women who were undecided about their committee preferences were subjected to "channeling," but they did not find this direction bothersome.

> As I looked at the list of what there was I knew that I wasn't qualified for anything, and I talked with a friend of mine . . . who was a legislator and a well-respected one, and he advised me to go on the Public Health and Welfare because of my concern for people.

This legislator felt that she had very definitely been directed toward her assignment because she was a woman, but she was perfectly well pleased: "Yes, because I think that in the field of health and welfare . . . I think that for a woman this is where she is at home." Another woman in doubt said:

> I was undecided. . . . There were several I was interested in, and I just simply couldn't take them all on, and so it was kind of hard choosing. . . . It came down to a choice be-

tween Elections and Public Health, and I was *urged just a little bit to take the one that would be more suitable for a woman.*

These "positive" expectations are linked to a set of "negative" expectations or proscriptions about what women are not interested in: "On certain matters we're not supposed to know as much as the men." And here again the expectation is not misplaced. "Well, the idea is that they know more of the business world. . . . It could be. The number of women involved in that kind of activity has never been as great as men." Female legislators' interest and expertise in health and welfare matters are not only a result of expectations of what they should be interested in, but are also a logical outgrowth of the actual prelegislative experience many of them have had—jobs in nursing, volunteer work, or social work. Similarly, women know little about "business" matters not simply because they are not expected to be interested in such things, but also because very few of them have had experience in them. Obviously the stereotypes to some degree determine the experiences, which in turn reinforce the stereotypes.

But what happens to the female legislator who has somehow missed the proper cues along the way? A former economics teacher remarks:

Women are not supposed to be interested in such hard issues as fiscal policy and this sort of thing which I am very interested in. . . . If someone else knew as much as I did about fiscal policy he would be more effective.

A woman lawyer in the New York legislature expresses similar sentiments:

Not only does a woman as a legislator have to get beyond the initial problems that everyone has to face as a new legislator of inexperience, but you have to *convince people that your legitimacy is more than just legitimacy as a woman* but rather as an individual human being and you have a capacity to handle any issue. So I say, "Come on, as much as you, Mr. So-And-So, have a capacity to handle these issues, so do I." *I'm not just limited in my scope to women's issues*—I'm not just limited in my scope to dealing with widows and children.

These women share the problem of having to deal with a set of stereotypical expectations about what they should be interested in that does not coincide with their own personal interests. Each of them resolved the conflict situation by acting on her own expectations—in effect attempting to prove to her colleagues that a woman can have expertise beyond the range of traditionally defined women's issues. This phenomenon of female legislators having to "prove themselves" was not limited to the particular individuals who wanted to establish themselves in nonfeminine issue areas, for several of the women reported feelings that they had to "prove" that they were competent legislators, irrespective of specific issue areas.

I don't know whether this is a fact or not, but I feel that women have to work harder to gain the respect of their colleagues. . . . If you want the job, prove that you can do it.

I have said over the years, and my colleagues here were debating it and saying it wasn't true, and I say, "But I've felt it." If you are a *male* they assume that you are *able until* you *prove youself incompetent.* With a *woman* it is *just the opposite.* They put you down as being not anybody to be reckoned with until you make it known that you have some brains and judgment.

I think that Ella Grasso [former Connecticut legislator now governor] has earned totally equal respect. I truly believe that. And I think that Gloria Schaffer [now secretary of the state in Connecticut] has earned totally equal respect. They did it—they stuck with it and I think they are treated completely as equals. So there are cases where this can be done. But it's *sort of like being black: in order to be equal you have to be so much better than anybody else in the world, and that is not equality.*

I think it took me longer to build up credibility with a group because I was a woman, and I felt that it was at first, you know, "She is a woman; what does she know?" So that is why I just made myself go out. I didn't want to just sit with the women in the lounge.

If there's only two like in here [New Hampshire senate] I think you have to *do your job overly well* because you're being looked at. They all listen more attentively when we speak.

Q: [several questions later] *What kind of advice would you give another woman who was just starting out in politics?*

A: She should go into it knowing that she has to *prove herself doubly* because she is a woman.

These legislators are all conscious of the salience of sex roles. They perceived conflicting expectations between how a woman should act and how a legislator should act. Moreover, they all apparently resolved the conflict by choosing the legislative, or professional, role. A vivid contrast with these women is provided by the following legislator's perceptions:

Q: *Have you ever felt that you had to work harder to prove yourself because you are a woman?*

A: No.

Q: *Have you had any difficulties establishing your credibility because you are a woman?*

A: I don't feel that I have, no. Of course, I am not that far out into things.

Q: *What do you mean, you are not that far out into things?*

A: Well, you know, really getting in there and plugging for this and that.

The feeling of "having to prove yourself" is experienced only if the female legislator wishes to become actively involved in the legislature. This last-quoted legislator probably had some awareness of the conflicting expectations, but readily resolved the situation by adopting the feminine role.

Not surprisingly, the phenomenon of women having to prove themselves is not limited to politics. Epstein reports the same phenomenon in her interviews with women in professions:

> Women in professions often asserted that they spent more time on work than a man would because they "must be better than a man". . . . They are all conscious of a special need to prove themselves and agree that this need continues throughout the professional career. Such an attitude, and its attendant *compulsive behavior* and overconformity reactions, are *typical* of strivers in *blocked opportunity structures*.

Epstein also reports that some of the women admitted that they resorted at times to using their "feminine qualities" in order to achieve their professional goals.

> They admit to flirting to attract attention or to persuade when the dispassionate approach fails. It is clear that most women in professional life disapprove of this, even though they may use it from time to time.[37]

In response to questions designed to see whether or not female legislators ever made use of such tactics, many of the legislators reacted with a curt no. However, the responses indicated that perhaps there were some who made use of such techniques. To the question, "Are there any particular tactics or strategies you can employ in achieving your legislative aims which are not available to male legislators?' " one woman responded,

> I suppose I could if I wanted to—exploit as a woman—but I don't do those things.
> Q: *Are there women who do?*
> A: Oh, I think so.
> Q: *Could you describe such a situation?*
> A: No, I really couldn't. I don't know how [considerable stumbling for words]. I don't mean to be prudish, but I don't feel that I have to shine up to a man to get him to vote

for anything. If the thing doesn't have merit, I'm not going to exploit myself to get the man to think that he's going to get something and vote for that issue. I think there are a few people who would do that.

To the same question another legislator replied,

No, unless you want to use women's wiles, which I'm afraid I don't know that much about.
Q: *Do you think there are women who try to do this sort of thing in order to get what they want on an issue?*
A: Actually there might be one or two. I can't say it is always successful.

Attempting to explore sensitive areas such as this through personal interviews leads to an awareness of the limitations of the interview technique as a research tool. Although there is no firm evidence that female legislators react to "blocked opportunity structures" by resorting to so-called "feminine wiles," there is considerable evidence that women are somewhat compulsive about carrying out their legislative tasks. The references to the conscientiousness of the average woman legislator were so frequent that the remarks cannot be dismissed as self-serving rationalizations or rampant female chauvinism. Is this conscientiousness a response to blocked opportunity structures, as suggested by Epstein and other sociologists? Unfortunately, the relationship does not appear to be that simple: the feeling of "having to prove yourself" was actually reported by only a minority of the female legislators, and several others when questioned about this phenomenon denied its existence. Yet conscientiousness appeared to be a behavior pattern that was shared almost universally among the women. There was considerable emphasis on "doing your homework." Although one would not want to infer that this practice is followed by all the female legislators, here is an indication of the seriousness with which one legislator takes her tasks:

I make it a rule before I go to bed every night to read every single thing that will be coming up the next day so I won't be blank on anything—so I won't ask any questions that show I haven't read anything, which sometimes happens [with the men].

Is it possible that conscientiousness—basic to the behavior pattern of most of the female legislators—is a response to the expectation that women are incompetent unless they prove otherwise, but that the expectation itself is often not consciously perceived? Is it their way of adapting to their "marginal man" status in the legislature? Or is it an outgrowth of sex-role training, a manifestation of the "tidy housewife" syndrome? Yet a third explanation might be something that was touched upon earlier, the fact that these women actually have fewer outside conflicts in the allocation of their time than male breadwinners. The question needs further exploration.

This phenomenon of "proving yourself" is manifested in various ways. Several of the women felt that in order to function effectively as legislators and be accepted by their male colleagues they had to disassociate themselves from certain stereotypes about female behavior.

I think perhaps they [women] have to be more logical than you would expect another fellow to be because there may be a bit of a hangover of the idea that women are emotional, and so you may have to be a *little more logical* to overcome the possibility of being accused of emotionalism.

I don't make any big pitches because I still feel that to be unemotional and logical is—I try to *appeal* to people *through logic*. That is the best way to do it.

Maybe that is one reason that I have had as much success as I do, because I have always deliberately *tried not to behave as a woman* but just as a senator.

We have a couple of women legislators in this house who will never be effective.
Q: *Why?*
A: Because they didn't learn to keep their mouths shut.

> From the very first day the legislative session opened they
> had to be down at that mike *making a lot of noise and*
> *sounding like women.*

It is evident that each of these legislators accepts the conventional stereotypes about women, for their concern about disprov-
ing the stereotypes goes no further than demonstrating that
they are the exceptions to their male colleagues' basically sound
expectations about female behavior. As might be expected,
these women can demonstrate considerable disdain for other
women: [38]

> They allow themselves to be second-class citizens. They
> allow themselves to be kept in these inferior positions. . . .
> I don't see why they allow themselves to be held back.

Helen Hacker, in a now classic comparative analysis of the behavior patterns of Negroes and women, identified what she
termed "minority-group self-hatred," which stems from the subordinate group's complete acceptance of the stereotyped concepts of itself held by the dominant group.[39] Epstein found that
group disparagement was not untypical among women professionals.[40] Several of the women in the present study, in particular those who explicitly engaged in group disparagement, used
men as their reference group. One legislator proudly reported,
"I've been told I think like a man." Another recounted this incident:

> I have always thought of myself as *more of a person than a*
> *woman* right from the beginning, and I have always been
> treated that way in our town. In fact the leader of the op-
> position years ago made some comment to the effect that *I*
> *thought like a man.* He made some comment, "behind
> those big brown eyes there lies"—how did he say it—"a
> conniving political mind, just like a man's . . ." The whole
> gist of the thing was that he felt that the opposition was on
> his level. [after further probing] Well, I thought it was a
> great compliment to me. He was implying that I wasn't
> making use of femininity particularly and that I was *think-*

ing on his level as far as reasons go. . . . I always try to keep everything on a reasonable basis rather than an emotional level.

Given the higher valuation of behavior patterns identified as masculine in this society, female legislators might be expected to use these patterns as a reference point for their own behavior. Female legislators, or any other women who have achieved certain status attributes traditionally associated with the dominant group in society, are in a situation of "status disequilibrium." Such women, having attained their status via universally accepted achievement techniques—as opposed to women who use their "charm" or other feminine qualities to gain a marital partner who brings them status—will probably respond to this situation of disequilibrium by orienting themselves toward male criteria of evaluation. This is not to say that all female legislators will respond to their situation in the same fashion; there is still, at least at this stage in the development of sex-role differentiation, considerable variation in role conceptions (this will be dealt with shortly). However, Galtung's more general work on status disequilibrium does suggest that many women who have achieved will use males as their reference group.[41]

One final note on the matter of stereotypes. I have essentially been dealing with how female legislators handle some of the conventional expectations about women. Unfortunately, the interviews cannot provide a direct test of how male legislators use these stereotypes in interactions with female colleagues; the following response is, however, suggestive:

Once, a male legislator turned to me and said, "Why don't you start thinking instead of voting off the top of your head!" But there again it was because we were on opposite sides.

Q: *Do you feel he said that because you are a woman?*
A: Both—could be. I don't know. It did happen to me.

Admittedly there is absolutely no evidence to indicate that the legislator would not have said the same thing to a man. But if we assume, for the purpose of generating fruitful hypotheses, that he fell back on this tactic because his opponent was a woman, it can by hypothesized that for at least some male legislators the traditional stereotypes provide a convenient tool for not dealing with the merits of an opposing point of view. The conventional culture provides a ready rationalization for dealing with displeasing arguments put forth by women. "Well, we know women can't think logically." A woman legislator who feels that women are freer to push for unpopular issues during a campaign remarks, "A woman can be free: she is of course discounted as not knowing any better and isn't it nice that her husband puts up with her." Another woman remarks: "People excuse the positions I take because I am a woman. They say, 'Oh well, you know, that's _____, that's O.K.' " In all three situations men were able to conveniently dismiss the substance of unwelcome arguments. However, in the first case there is the possibility of another dimension: perhaps the male legislator's verbal assault is not merely a device to restore his own cognitive balance but is also intended to put the woman on the defensive—"Come on now, you're falling back on sloppy feminine thinking; act like a legislator!"—and force her to drop her position. Once again, there is need for further exploration.

Much of the discussion up to now has been a description of the "burdens" or special demands encountered by the female legislator in her role relationship with male colleagues. However, role relationships also can involve opportunities (certainly the case vis-à-vis constituents), and for at least some of the women there was a feeling that their status as women afforded them certain opportunities which increased their legislative effectiveness.

The men are very gentlemanly with you. They will open a door, help you with your coat, or—they seem to have a sense that you are a woman and that you should be treated as a woman. They also have a sense that you are *a woman and you don't know anything*. You don't know as much as they do. But if you handle things carefully by not overstep-

ping and fooling around and just get little points across here and there, I find that you can use it to an advantage.
Q: *Could you describe a situation where you have been able to do this?*
A [describes encounters while trying to draft a bill]: You can ask questions and get answers. *You can be more direct.* With the commissioner of safety I was—*a man might not be as rude as I was.* I just came right out and said what I wanted. . . . When I left I'm not sure he thought I was going along with everything he said, but I knew I wasn't; but I left him that way to keep him off guard. I feel that if you work it around the men seem to, well, maybe they do listen to you more than they might listen to another man. I don't know—I just have this feeling that as a woman *I can get around things just a little bit more* than a man can.

I have a great reputation for—you know, we have these hearings, and I'm supposed to be a commissioner-hater because I put very *awkward questions* to them and I pin them down. And many times my colleagues have said: "You know we wouldn't dare ask the questions you do. *Because you're a woman you can get away with it.*" I resent this. It may be true because I can be a littler gentler in the way I phrase it, but I don't like to think it is and I never did that on purpose—except perhaps as a woman does have a certain relationship with men so that she can do things a little joking.

Each of these women feels that colleagues and other men encountered in a professional context relate to female legislators in a way that affords the women maneuverability: for example, they can obtain information that a male legislator in a similar situation might not be able to obtain. The relevant question is, why do male legislators grant female legislators this extra room?

Q: *Has being a woman ever helped?*
A: Oh, I don't know. Well, the way some men still react to women, they would rather keep them happy than put up

with their fussing [laughs]. I think that sometimes, in committee, some men may say, "Let's give it to her and keep
her quiet."

The traditional courtesies color the style of interaction in the
legislative arena as well as in the campaign. A woman who is
sensitive to this reality and also confident about her legislative
abilities can use this to her advantage in certain contexts. It is
true that the courtesies accorded women are a derivative of the
cultural norm that women need to be protected: the dominant
and superior group shall have the responsibility of caring for the
subordinate and weaker group. But because the rituals themselves are such a basic part of social conditioning, for at least
some men they are basic reflex responses without conscious
feelings of intense condescension. We might hypothesize, then,
that the positive opportunities afforded women legislators by such
courtesies depend on the degree of condescension permeating
the situation. If the condescension is limited, courtesies can
provide certain short-run or limited advantages (why the advantages are only short-run will be dealt with later). Just as the
women have varying responses to the traditional expectations,
so do the men; male legislators are not an undifferentiated
mass.

> There are very few women, and that is very important.
> Therefore each woman kind of stands out as somebody a
> little bit different, and somebody you don't get up and at
> tack on the floor, and you don't undercut in quite the way
> you do a man. It is a very positive thing there. I found that I
> got a lot of special help on a lot of difficult bills, and I got
> every one of my bills through. And I believe it had a lot to
> do with being a woman.

When a woman legislator breaks one of the rules of the game
which presumably applies to all legislators—for example, the
norm that members will not waste their colleagues' time talking
unnecessarily—sanctions are not imposed as readily on the female "offender" as on a man. Several of the legislators felt that

if a woman gets up on the floor and rambles on at length, it is more likely that she will "get away with it." It is not that she is afforded a special opportunity to be effective, but simply that traditional sanctions are less likely to be imposed. However, women are probably granted this "luxury" only because their speaking habits are such that allowing women to violate the norm does not seriously impede the expeditious flow of legislative business.

Female legislators in Connecticut and New Hampshire generally do not speak as much on the floor of the assembly as do male legislators. The reason for this is complex. For one thing, very few of the women are leaders, and several of the women pointed to this as a contributing factor. But there also appears to be a degree of reluctance, on the part of some women, simply because of the size of the body. In New Hampshire there were several references to the fact that although women might speak less on the floor, they hold their own ground in committee. It is more than likely that, particularly in New Hampshire, this discrepancy in behavior also is true of many male legislators. The possibility that women speak less because they are responding to some expectation about female behavior was touched on by one legislator in Connecticut, who noted that women get a "very attentive" audience reception because they do not speak very often. But she added, "If you speak too much I think they think you are not demure enough or something—there is that problem." Several of the women in New Hamsphire noted that there was a very practical reason for a woman not to speak on the floor:

> Women can be a lot more effective in committee, only because on the *floor* your *voice* comes out *shriller over the mike*. A woman does speak better in committee.

But probably the main reason sanctions are not imposed on the female legislator when she speaks at length is not that women speak less frequently but that when they do speak they rarely waste other members' time:

I think that men like to talk, despite what they say about
women. Women get up and speak, but I think they say
what they want to say and that is it. Very often men will really get carried away with their own speeches.
Women can put their point across maybe a little more
clearly.
Q: *Why is this so?*
A: They just don't go around the bush. They come out
with the facts. They are quite sharp and to the point. They
don't get up and go on and on like some of the men do.

The explanation for women's relative brevity in their presenta-
tions was quite aptly put together by one legislator in Connecticut:

You see, this is a beautiful stepping-stone, let's say for a
very ambitious attorney. Some day he might be a judge.
These things are very evident if you would see the performance. I do. I feel this very deeply in watching and listen-
ing to them get up and emoting and performing on the floor
of the house and going off on a big long tangent on something. I feel it is quite unnecessary, but when you think of
what they've got at stake you can understand. *I myself have
nothing to look forward to; I'm not interested in being a
judge or anything else. I'm just up here to do a job as a
legislator.* These traits come out more so in men than in
women; there isn't a woman in this house that acts like
that.

This woman in her own words has stated the essence of Joseph
A. Schlesinger's theory of political ambition: "The central assumption of ambition theory is that a politician's behavior is a
response to his office goals." [42] In *The Lawmakers* James Barber
describes a type of legislator which he dubs the "Advertiser."
The Advertiser is a "limelighter" who frequently speaks because
his "primary focus of attention is not on the softer reward of
good fellowship but on the use he can make of political office for
his own advancement." [43] An interest in self-advancement is

not an important motivating factor for the average female legislator in Connecticut and New Hampshire. In fact, for several of
them there is a distinct self-consciousness about any action in
which they might appear to be promoting themselves.

> I think anything you do has an impact; hopefully it's un-
> conscious to you.

> There are people who are very ambitious to get places and
> do a lot of selling. I don't think this is necessarily the way to
> get the thing you're interested in. If what you want is re-
> sults and you're not interested in credit you make great
> progress.

> I work for the people all the time. You build your image bit
> by bit—not on purpose.

Historically the role of women has been to provide the necessary
support so that males could go out and achieve. Women who
have been conditioned to derive their identity from what they
can do for others are not likely to drop this predisposition when
they move out of the home. Moreover, women's outside activities have generally been in the so-called "helping fields"—nursing, social work, teaching of young children—and so it is to be
expected that this would be their orientation in political jobs.

To return to the matter of opportunities afforded women via
the traditional courtesies: the female legislator's sex status un-
deniably can, in certain contexts, provide limited advantages.
However, access to these few advantages comes at a price, for
female legislators must fulfill certain expectations about how
women should behave. Generally male legislators do not directly
undercut female legislators, but this privilege is based on the
expectation that a woman will not retaliate against her colleagues. "Of course our instinct is not to. I really believe that.
But I don't think you do. You don't lose your temper—except
maybe occasionally." And according to this one legislator, when
a woman does break these norms she loses respect.

> The other counterpart of being a woman is that there is
> that sort of respect for you as a sincere, nonpolitical type,

and if you are losing your temper or going around sort of acting like the men, in a way this can hurt you. It is a very fine line there, but men do expect you not to be tough and threatening or angry.

A legislator in New York refers to this same dilemma:

So when you start from scratch I think the natural kind of inclination is if you're friendly and responsible and reasonably charming, it can be an asset just because they don't mind having you around in that way. If you begin to start looking for some of the same kind of power to accomplish things, then you may be labeled aggressive, and then they don't like that very well, and that happens.

On the other hand, although men may be displeased when they perceive a female legislator as aggressive, her legislative effectiveness need not be utterly destroyed. As one legislator put it, she has to be that much more clever politically. Although the data here do not permit systematic analysis of the consequences of various tactics, a situation in New Hampshire is suggestive. When I queried legislators there as to whether they had ever been accused of being aggressive or heard such remarks about a female colleague, there were repeated references to a particular situation. After my own observations it soon became clear that all the remarks concerned one legislator who had a stride that was "not exactly feminine."

I have heard it said about _____. They have said she ought to act more feminine. The problem with _____ is they're afraid of her. She's very aggressive, very intelligent, taught state and local government and probably knows more about it than 99 percent of the people here. She's a chairman. [Executive Departments and Administration—not a typical committee for a female legislator.] She likes to see things get done, she frequently wears pants suits, and she has a stride that's not exactly feminine. Men become uptight with her and consequently pick up on these aspects. Nothing to her face—a lot of whispering and comments when she walks out of the room.

All the legislators seemed to agree that despite all the remarks this woman was extremely effective. A plausible explanation might be one of the following: (1) this legislator is tolerated because of the very real lack of available talent in the New Hampshire legislature; (2) the remarks themselves enable the males to overcome their discomfort about her lack of proper feminine behavior, allowing them to focus on her status as a legislator; or perhaps (3) sanctions have been imposed which curtail her effectiveness, for, if she is as talented as she is reputed to be, should she not be in an even more powerful position? The questions posed by this situation warrant systematic exploration.

Lobbyists

The female legislator's interactions with lobbyists seem to be affected by her sex status to a greater extent than her interactions with any other of her legislative role partners. This finding accords with previous research on lobbying which indicated that there was considerable variation in legislators' orientations toward lobbyists and that these orientations had very real consequences for interactions.[44] Zeigler and Baer, in their study of the recruitment of lobbyists and legislators, found that legislators who were more acculturated to the "give-and-take" of politics were more likely to interact with lobbyists.[45] Females are not socialized for careers in politics—this has been repeatedly emphasized throughout this study—but certain aspects of traditional sex-role training are probably more transferable to politics than others. There is very little in the traditional training for women that is readily transferable to the give-and-take aspect of politics. Thus it is unlikely that female legislators would be positively disposed to this dimension, and moreover the large majority of these women did not even have the kinds of prelegislative experience that might acculturate them to such an orientation. In fact, an "anti-politics" posture was prevalent among them. Typical were such comments as "not interested in mechanics of politics," "don't like the political bargaining," "It's really government that I am interested in, not politics." This orientation in large part accounts for the following kind of response to queries about contact with lobbyists:

You hear about lobbyists. . . . I don't know where it is.

Lobbyists? I don't know them, because nobody has ever lobbied . . .

I stay clear of lobbyists.

Lobbyists don't approach women as much.

It is important to emphasize the independent effects of an "antipolitics" orientation. Legislators who have little information about lobbyists and are negatively disposed are not likely to interact frequently with them, irrespective of the legislators' sex status. As one legislator in New Hampshire put it, "Lobbyists do not approach me as much because they know I'm not here to be bought or changed, but they don't approach _____ [a male legislator who was chairman of this woman's committee] either."

Sex status is also relevant in the shaping of the lobbyists' initial expectations as to how legislators will respond to encounters: these expectations probably reflect a generalized image of women which basically corresponds with this legislator's image of herself:

I've tried to always give the *image* that I would *not be subject to the* persuasiveness of lobbyists. For this reason I don't think they have used any of the tempting snares to buy your vote.

A legislator in Connecticut describes the interactions between female legislators and lobbyists as follows:

Q: *What about lobbyists? Do lobbyists approach women?*
A: By and large not. Occasionally, but by and large not.
Q: *Less frequently?*
A: Less frequently.
Q: *Why do you think this is so?*
A: One, because we are *not interested in what they may*

have to offer, or whatever. Also, because they don't think we are that powerful anyway: so they will come to us after they have seen the important people.

Another Connecticut legislator notes,

I think lobbyists have a tendency to ignore the women, frankly.
Q: *Why do you think this is so?*
A: I think it may be just that they *think they can bat it out better with the men.*

Again,

They are wary of us because we don't put up with them.

In general women legislators are not approached as frequently as their male colleagues because lobbyists have certain expectations as to how women will react and believe that women do not "carry the weight." Neither of these expectations is entirely misplaced, because the women do pride themselves on being independent and resistant to pressure, and most women are not in powerful positions. A female legislator in Connecticut who was an assistant majority leader responded to a query about approaches by lobbyists rather indignantly with, "Absolutely! Just as much, of course!" She went on to add that the extent of lobbying depended on the particular committee and that she was sure she was approached as much as any male legislator in her position on the Insurance Committee. This suggests that the difference in lobbying activities vis-à-vis the sexes may be partially accounted for by the kinds of committees women serve on. Interest groups that concern themselves with the policy outputs of the Insurance and Real Estate Committee or the State and Urban Development Committee are more highly organized and better funded than comparable groups in the health and welfare area. Another factor that needs to be considered is the sex status of the lobbyists.

They don't ignore the women, but here again you know it is because *we don't frequent the same places.* Most of the lob-

byists are men anyway, and they have a tendency to chew
the fat in the corridors and converge in different places
together. . . . I think it is natural that they gravitate toward
the men in the assembly because *they feel more at ease
with them* probably.

The male legislators and the lobbyists are more likely to interact
simply because they have greater opportunities for informal
contact. Their social patterns both inside and outside of the
state house are more likely to intersect. In Connecticut, for example, women are not even allowed in the "Hawaiian Room," a
bar located in the state capitol building.[46] In addition, the male
legislator in his role as family breadwinner is part of an occupational network that may bring him into contact with lobbyists;
the female legislator's housewife role does not normally provide
such opportunities. Also, the more informal the setting, the
greater the possibility that there will be some feeling of impro-
priety about encounters between a male lobbyist and a female
legislator. In New Hampshire many of the women accept the
general invitations to the functions sponsored by the racetrack
lobby, but a female senator felt it was very difficult for her to
have lunch or dinner with lobbyists. She said that she always
arranges to have other people with her, whereas

the men don't have a second thought about it. I never
thought about it before until now. I know them [lobbyists]
all and like them all, but I don't run around.

For a variety of reasons the female legislator is less subject to
the arm-twisting of lobbyists than is her male colleague. But
previous research has indicated that lobbyists can also provide
needed information which assists the legislator in ac-
complishing legislative tasks. Is the effectiveness of the female
legislator curtailed because of her less frequent contact with
lobbyists? Although the feelings of individuals cannot be accepted as proof that there is no significant impact, none of the
female legislators felt that her effectiveness was in any way hindered. Several of those who were actively involved in legislative

activities mentioned that when they needed information from lobbyists they simply went and got it. A woman in New Hampshire recounted that she "picked a lobbyist's brain" in getting information for her housing bill. Only in New Hampshire were there female legislators who had had absolutely no contact with lobbyists. But this probably had as much to do with the general characteristics of the assembly as with sex status. Given the size of the assembly, there are probably many male legislators too who never interact with lobbyists. There also appears to be a fairly strong antilobbying orientation in New Hampshire, for lobbyists are not even allowed in the hallway between the house and senate chambers. The only place a lobbyist may talk to a legislator in the state house is a rather uninviting basement cafeteria; opportunities for formalized contacts, which minimize the obtrusiveness of sex status, are limited.

We have seen how the behavioral expectations associated with the feminine role affect the female legislator's interactions in the legislature. The impact of the other roles the female legislator is likely to hold also need to be considered. It was thought that the roles of mother and housewife would impose burdens on the female legislator's time. Much of the literature on the role problems of professional women has dealt with the role problems only in terms of allocation of time.[47] Among the women who were interviewed here, this factor turned out to be less of a problem than was expected, largely because of the nature of their family situatons. Very few of the women had young children; the years when the mother role is most demanding lay behind them. A legislator in Connecticut describes what factors she took into account in deciding to run for the legislature:

> *I had the time* and the family support. *I wouldn't have run when they were younger,* and I don't think that I would have wanted to. I always felt that a mother's first concern should be her family.

This attitude was fairly typical of the women whose children were grown. They felt that their pattern was the most appropriate one for all women. One legislator in Connecticut felt that

young women should not come to the legislature, not only because it would take time from their children but also because it
would show a lack of propriety:

> I don't think much of young women trying to come to the
> legislature. It takes too much time . . . and there are *too
> many men around here*. I've seen it many times. You know,
> you get mixed up with some other man. It just doesn't
> seem to work very well for women to come too young.

This legislator is making a moral judgment, but it cannot be
denied that normally when children are grown a woman's sex
status is less obtrusive than during the years when they are
young. Hence an older woman may very well have fewer problems deriving from her sex status than a younger woman.

> In most cases, as the woman ages her sexual appeal be-
> comes less an object of focus. Since a woman is apt to en-
> counter resistance if her professional status requires the ex-
> ercise of authority over others, she may find that she can
> depend on deriving a certain amount of authority from her
> age. While a man might resent "taking orders" from a
> woman, he probably would be less resistant if the woman is
> older.[48]

One legislator in Connecticut felt that she derived certain advantages from the "impression of being a conscientious grandmother." On the other hand, there are different problems for the
older woman. In Connecticut a woman in her late fifties, who
had been in the legislature for sixteen years, felt that since reapportionment they had "become a youthful legislature" and that
there now existed an age barrier. A woman legislator in New
York remarked that when the men get together to go to dinner
she does not feel free to join them: "But that is not only because
they're men but also most of them are much younger than I am
and have different interests than an old lady." Another related
consequence of delayed entrance into political life is that future
opportunities are eliminated before they are considered. Admittedly there are other shaping constraints limiting these women's

political ambitions, but age is clearly a basic limiting condition for women who first run for elective office when their children are grown. "Not having started younger, I don't have the ambition to seek higher office." A woman senator in New Hampshire, who remained politically active while her children were growing up, sums up the situation like this:

They hesitate. In the years that they would be good at it— late twenties and early thirties—they've got children at home and feel hemmed in, don't want anyone to think that they're not serving their family. This is the time that they'd be so good, and this is the time that they hesitate.

Whether a woman works her legislative career around her growing family or postpones it until the most burdensome years of motherhood are over, her family roles have very real consequences for the kinds of commitments she feels she can make to the legislature. A legislator in New Hampshire, whose children are grown, feels that the main presure confronting women in politics is the question of *the focus of primary loyalty.*

This is the reason that I'm not running again . . . my husband finds it disconcerting that I come in and the phone starts ringing and doesn't stop until it's time for bed. Although my children are grown and away from home—am I depriving my grandchildren of time that perhaps they should have?

A legislator in Connecticut attributed her divorce to the fact that legislative work had kept her away from home too much. Her response to the question, "How do you think you have done so far as a legislator?" was, "I think my family has suffered, and that is where it counts." One technique for reducing role strain is the reduction of role relationships.[49]

For many of the women role strain is reduced simply by limiting the commitment to their political careers—or limiting the scope of their involvement in the legislature.

I have *no political aspirations.* And here again it *may be particularly because of the family situation.* I am reaching a point where my husband is getting ready to begin to take more time off, and I am certainly going to be available to spend it with him. In a sense, this perhaps is one of the areas where *being a woman is changing my future* a little bit because I definitely prefer to be a member of the family unit rather than continuing on in this line.

A legislator in Connecticut who had been approached to run for Congress was hesitant about considering it because "it means going away from your family. . . . for the moment I think it is *too much for a woman to aspire to normally, and I'm still a little bit normal.*" A legislator in New Hampshire, who is chairman of the Education Committee, feels that because of family responsibilities she will have to step down from the chairmanship for the next session. She recounted: "My husband said to me, 'I don't think you should be chairman of the regular session next year,' and I said, 'No, I agree with you.'" A first-term legislator in Connecticut feels that she has been unable to accept certain responsibilities in the legislature because of her family obligations, even though her family is "all grown up."

This is difficult . . . because my husband would really like to see more of me, whereas I really could do a better job if I stayed up here at least three nights a week . . . but forget it—I really don't think my marriage could survive.

These women were all rather articulate about the extent to which their family responsibilities shaped the scope of their political involvement. There were, however, other legislators who did not see their family roles as limiting what they *wanted* to do in the legislature; they felt no strains because they had "a supportive husband" or because they "had help at home." Undoubtedly these conditions are necessary if the female legislator is to minimize the conflict between her family and legislative roles, but I have stressed the notion of "want" because for these women family roles have shaped their actual political wants, and therefore felt strain is minimal. It is no mere coincidence that the only female legislator in either state who was very interested in going on to higher office was unmarried. In general, legislators interviewed for this study experienced less role strain than was expected, but this finding is largely attributable to the nature of the legislative job in New Hampshire. Three of the female legislators in the assembly who had young children also had outside jobs in addition to their jobs in the legislature. These women were not "superwomen"; their ability to manage their role responsibilities without undue strain simply attests to the level of commitment required by the legislative role in New Hampshire. Here, in contrast to many other states, the legislative role does not make the kinds of demands on time and resources that involve a basic restructuring of an individual's other roles.[50]

The female legislator's family roles can also have an impact on the direction of her legislative interests and basic orientation. Although this was not the case with the majority of the legislators here, a husband's interest can be the reason for the initial political involvement: "My husband is very involved in politics . . . so by osmosis I've picked up all this gossip about politics." "My husband has been a fantastic influence simply because he is so interested in politics." One woman in New Hampshire ran for the legislature because her husband was unable to run again, and once she was elected she followed through on his interest in education (he was a school principal) by becoming actively involved in the Education Committee. Two women whose husbands were doctors developed an interest in the health field. One of these women felt that her mutual professional interest with her husband made for a "perfect natural relationship." Research on women in professions has suggested that role strain can be reduced when there is continuity between professional and private lives and that a couple working in the same field can provide such a situation.[51]

The economic support provided by a husband appears to have a subtle effect on the female legislator's basic orientation. Earlier I discussed the fact that many of the women prided themselves on being "independent." This attitude derives from a variety of factors, but some of the female legislators attributed their independence to their economic freedom:

The main advantage is that you in a very real way can be your real self. I think for many people their jobs and livelihood—well, their family's well-being—depend on their giving in to public opinion.

Women are very honest about their opinions and ideas . . . they have nothing to gain from being anything but honest . . . they're not looking for better positions.

Two women legislators in New York feel that more women should enter politics because they can afford to:

We're losing a lot of men because they just can't afford the job. Now women, those who have their children raised and can be away from home, if they have another wage earner in the household, are better able to handle some of the jobs that are not well paid.

We just desperately need people who have greater freedom than most of my colleagues have, and I mean economic freedom. The average woman who comes in is economically secure . . . she is *less subject to political pressures and economic pressures* than my colleagues.

The female legislator's economic independence provides her with the opportunity to be politically independent (though, as discussed earlier, there are other factors that push her in this direction). Freedom from the role of family breadwinner also explains the conscientiousness of the average female legislator:

Women are very conscientious about attending and doing their job. And they perhaps have *less to divert them*, whereas men are in business or in law.

It isn't that I am anything special, but I am conscientious . . . *I have the time* where the *men who have to earn their living don't.*

Once a woman decides to take on the legislative role, she can often allocate more of her time and resources to legislative duties than a male legislator, who also has the role of family breadwinner. Although the evidence is indirect, it does not appear that the female legislator is generally subject to more private-versus-public role strain than the male legislator—at least with regard to the allocation of time. In legislatures like Connecticut and New Hampshire, *it is absolutely impossible*—no matter how well-intentioned the legislator may be—to fulfill the requirements of the family breadwinner role while relying solely on the salary provided by the legislature. The breadwinner-legislator is not as protected from role strain as the ordinary male professional, because the environment does not provide a clear hierarchy of values as to how he should allocate his time between the legislature and his occupation. A female legislator in New Hampshire summed the situation up quite well: "People like a woman candidate—they know she'll be there."

5: Benchwarming and Beyond

In this chapter we turn more directly to the question of personal role definition: *How do individual women legislators orient themselves to the parts they play in the legislature?* So far we have mapped out the environment or "socio-psychological world" faced by the female legislator. The description of this environment made clear that various legislators develop different modes of adaptation. Confronted with a complex system of expectations and conditions of work, individuals work out their personal role definitions. Role definitions need to be dealt with more systematically, because various modes of adaptation may have important consequences both for the functioning of the legislature as an institution and for the overall status of women in society. "Personal role definition . . . may serve in various ways to maintain or change the social structure." [1] I shall delineate here the variables that differentiate the various role conceptions. This task will be essentially descriptive: in each case the pattern of recruitment, level of self-commitment, mode of activity, and perception of sex-role salience are examined. The implications of each type for the institution and its policy outputs are dealt with subsequently. The development of the typology was heavily dependent on the interviews with female legislators from New York—for it is clear that personal role conceptions are a function of the structural demands of the legislature as well as personality variables, and consequently the distribution of role conceptions within a given legislature is dependent on the structural context. [2]

The Modal Types: Personal Role
Definitions of Female Legislators

It is possible to identify four distinct patterns of adaptation to the legislative environment on the part of the female legislators. This typology was developed in the context of state legislatures, but I believe the categories themselves can be used to explain the behavior of female political elites in other institutions. The typology is based on the interaction of two distinct variables, and my contention is that once this pair of factors is known, predictions can be made as to how a female legislator is likely to react in various settings. The two variables that define the basic categories are self-image and attitude toward women's role in society. In general women have lower self-evaluations than men, a predictable outgrowth of sex-role training and the valuation of the sexes by society.[3] "A sense of worthlessness seems to be fairly widespread among women."[4] Negative self-image in large part explains why so few women even enter politics, where a positive assertion of the self is generally a prerequisite for success. However, as has been shown throughout this study, neither sex is of one mold, and women do vary considerably along this dimension. One might think that only a woman with a very positive self-image could overcome all the barriers that beset a woman interested in a career in politics, and if leadership selection were simply a matter of self-selection this might very well be the case. However, leadership recruitment is also a function of environmental conditions: as has been demonstrated here and in other studies, recruitment can sometimes be a matter of "who is available." Consequently there is considerable variation in self-image even among female political elites. The historical evidence makes it clear that there have always been women interested in changing women's role in society; but the research here was conducted during a period when the interest in such change was sufficiently widespread to constitute a social movement. The existence of such a mass movement, in a period when the communications media have a profound influence on life-styles and values, is of considerable importance for the interaction between self-image and attitude toward women's role in society. Although firm empirical evidence is lacking, I think it probable that the women who have been most concerned about changing women's role in society and have taken some initiative in trying to effect change have in general had relatively positive self-images. This hypothesis is derived from the expansion of two ideas previously discussed. For a woman to feel frustrated with her sex role, she must consider it legitimate to compare it with that of the opposite sex. But she is likely to have such a feeling only if she has achieved status attributes normally associated with men. And women who have achieved are likely to have relatively positive self-images. Such women will be the ones to initiate attempts at change (they also have some of the requisite resources, such as time, education, and money). But once the individual efforts generate a movement, the values of these women will spread, and the ideas themselves will have an influence on women who have not achieved and do not have positive self-images. Such women may adopt the notion that women's role in society needs to be changed, while at the same time retaining their negative self-images. Self-evaluations which evolve out of early childhood experience are probably less subject to change than more general attitudes about the functioning of society. Although I had originally predicted that such women would be so negative in their assessment of themselves and of women's role in society that they would not be found in the legislature, close examination of the data indicates that, given certain environmental conditions, this role type may nevertheless exist there.

Table 5.1 indicates the different role types predicted by the interaction between the two variables. These categories are presented as ideal types for the purpose of explanation; both common sense and the interview data indicate that actual role conceptions of individual legislators fall along the two continua, but for the purpose of conceptual clarity these variables are best dealt with as dichotomous. For each category several legislators who best exemplify each type are examined. In order not to give an illusion of false precision, I want to stress that assignment to

Table 5.1 Legislative Role Types

	Attitude toward Women's Present Role in Society	
Self-Image	*Negative* (*change needed*)	*Positive* (*no change needed*)
Negative	Passive Women's Rights Advocate	Housewife-Benchwarmer
Positive	Women's Rights Advocate	Traditional Civic Worker

the four categories was made simply on the basis of perceived patterns gleaned from a close and sober reading of the transcripts.

Housewife-Benchwarmer

The Housewife-Benchwarmer is fairly common in the New Hampshire assembly and much less common in the Connecticut assembly. Seven out of the eleven women interviewed in New Hampshire were so classified, compared to only two out of the eight women interviewed in the Connecticut assembly. Although I am hesitant to say that these percentages reflect the actual proportions of Housewife-Benchwarmers in each assembly, they probably give a reasonably close approximation. Prior to reapportionment the percentage of Housewife-Benchwarmers among Connecticut's female legislators was probably much higher. It is significant that the two women who were classified as Housewife-Benchwarmers in the Connecticut assembly were the two who had the longest tenure (five and eight terms); they alone had begun their careers in the assembly prior to reapportionment. The Housewife-Benchwarmer, in fact, acts in much the same way as James Barber's "Spectator." Barber, it should be recalled, conducted his interviews during a pre-reapportionment legislative session (1959), and a large proportion of the legislators classified as Spectators were housewives.[5] One might well ask if the Housewife-Benchwarmer is but a historical curiosity. Barber says of the Spectator: "It is difficult to predict how long the Spectator will last as a legislator. One suspects . . . the place would eventually begin to pall on him." [6] In Connecticut, and probably most other states, the Housewife-Benchwarmer may very well be a legislative type that is vanishing. But this is not the case in New Hampshire, and it is not likely to become the case unless the mammoth New Hampshire assembly is drastically reduced in size. Considering that more female legislators have served and do serve in New Hampshire than in any other state, examination of the Housewife-Benchwarmer is a matter of more than antiquarian interest.

The Housewife-Benchwarmer has a fairly negative self-image and is basically content with women's present role in society. She is certainly not interested in any basic changes in the division of labor between the sexes. Plagued by self-doubt, with little confidence in her abilities, she is in the legislature only because she comes from a district where there is no competition for the nomination. Often she is actually beseeched to run because nobody else will.

> Someone called at five in the afternoon and said no one is running for representative; why don't you run? I said I couldn't—in the first place I don't know enough, and in the second place *the thought frightens me.*

> The person who was the representative had decided not to run, and the townspeople came and asked me if I would take over. I ran unopposed, and here I am.
> Q: *How did you feel about the idea when it was suggested to you?*
> A: I was really very . . . oh, what is the word—*unhappy about it.* I really didn't want to do it.
> Q: *Then why did you run?*
> A: Because otherwise the town would have been unrepresented. . . .
> Q: *In making up your mind about running, what factors did you take into account? What were some of the pros and cons?*

A: Well, the cons first . . . that I *would be inadequate.* I knew nothing about the inner workings of politics.

. . . eventually I was asked to run for the state legislature.
Q: *Who asked you to run?*
A: The same group of friends that I knew, and I had no intention of running for anything in the state. . . . I said, "Oh, I *couldn't possibly do that.*" But they worked on me a while and I came around.

This legislator ran because she could not find anyone else to run and the slate had to be filled. She describes her feelings about running this way:

I *dreaded* it. I had no concept of what I was going to get into. . . . I had the *time to spare* because I was a housewife.

The Housewife-Benchwarmer, like the Spectator, reaches the legislature because she is an available volunteer.[7] Not surprisingly, she also has absolutely no political ambitions. "No" was the typical response to the query, "Are you interested in running for any other offices?":

I do not feel that I am capable of holding a higher office.
. . . I haven't got the education, and I don't feel that I'm knowledgeable enough in government—so why should I step forward when I'm a novice in what I'm doing now?

. . . No desire to go any higher. I'm not qualified.

The Housewife-Benchwarmer may be happy with her present legislative role even though she did not strive for it, but she certainly does not aspire to anything beyond the assembly. She does not have progressive political ambitions.[8] This lack of ambition among female legislators was noted earlier, and there are a variety of factors accounting for it. For the Housewife-Benchwarmer her self-image is a critical factor: she feels she simply does not have what it takes. Also, her degree of commitment to politics is minimal. One Housewife-Benchwarmer offered her advice to other women interested in politics: "The main thing is doing what you feel called to do, and it doesn't have to be a forever thing." A limited commitment to politics among many female legislators was noted before. For the Housewife-Benchwarmer it stems primarily from doubts about her abilities and her commitment to the traditional division of labor between the sexes, but the low level of risk in running for a legislative seat in her district is a third factor. Given the relatively small size of the districts (2,000–4,000 in New Hampshire and 18,000–20,000 in Connecticut) and the minimal level of competition, her net investment in running for the seat does not require much of a commitment to politics.[9] It is actually only because the costs— campaign funds, time, energy, and so forth—are so minimal that the Housewife-Benchwarmer is in the legislature at all. She would not be there if the required investments were greater because of her aforementioned self-doubt and traditional view of sex roles: "I don't think a woman has the time to campaign, and to tell the truth I wouldn't know how to campaign." * Such a woman is not interested in seeing any fundamental changes in the division of labor between the sexes either in society at large or in her own personal situation, for she is happy with the present allocation of roles and in fact feels rather positive about women's role in society:

> I have always felt that I enjoyed the role of a woman. It hasn't bothered me one way or the other . . . about not being equal or something or other. I don't even care to be equal. I think we have our own role and that we are just as important in every sense of the word, and more so. . . .

> I guess I don't like the feeling that girls can take over completely as far as men are concerned. I think that she will find in later years that she is better off if she is married and she does have a family and they work together rather than trying to go it alone.

---

* We noted earlier that the number of Housewife-Benchwarmers has probably decreased in Connecticut since reapportionment.

I'll tell you, there are a lot of things that I thoroughly enjoy about being a woman—courtesies paid to me by other people. I enjoy having a man hold my coat while I put it on; I don't care whether it is that he feels that I'm not capable of doing it . . . the same if a man opens a door for a woman.

I would hate to think that we're on the same par with men and that the little courtesies that men have shown women would be forgotten. I like to have a man open the car door, hold my coat. . . .

Given her feelings about women's role in society, the House-wife-Benchwarmer's primary commitment is predictably to her family. The demands she experiences there totally shape whatever commitments she makes to the legislature. This is how the Housewife-Benchwarmer responds to the question about possible conflict between being a woman and being a legislator:

Well, being away from home—my husband has to be very lenient with me. . . . He's very understanding and kind. But it is a little bit different for a man than for a woman, I think. You expect a man . . . that is his business. But I don't honestly know as you would call this [long pause]. . . . No, *I'm still a housewife, and really that comes first.* And it does interfere a little bit.

My primary obligation is always at home.

The only thing that women in politics have are the pressures of where does your primary loyalty remain, and I speak of this for the very reason that I'm not running again.

Now very often I have felt I had to go home because my husband wanted dinner, or when he wasn't feeling well I thought I should be home. And with a man it is not quite the same thing; he is out in the world anyway. But *a woman is expected to have something to do with her home, and I approve of that.*

Actually the Housewife-Benchwarmer often had little or no response to questions designed to test whether the legislator perceived conflicting role expectations. She also generally had few responses to questions designed to gauge the legislator's awareness of the extent to which sex determined the allocation of roles and responsibilities in the legislature. This reticence is in line with the original hypothesis, which stated that there was a relationship between consciousness of the salience of sex roles and the experience of role conflict. Because the Housewife-Benchwarmer accepts virtually without question the present role of women in society, she is not consciously aware of the extent to which sex roles determine behavior.

> Q: *Have you ever felt that you were not considered for a particular committee post or position of leadership because you were a woman?*
> A: Well, no, I haven't thought of it that way.

Awareness of the salience of sex roles comes about only when one is frustrated with one's own sex role, and such frustration presupposes the legitimacy of comparing one's role with that of the opposite sex. The Housewife-Benchwarmer's life experiences have been so different from those of the average man that she does not find it very meaningful to compare roles. Only one of the Housewife-Benchwarmers had completed college, and any occupational or political involvements she had were peripheral to the center of her life—her family.

Once she is in the assembly the Housewife-Benchwarmer's mode of activity is conditioned by her self-doubts and her attitude toward women's role in society. She accepts many of the traditional stereotypes without question.

> Q: *Do you think there are any particular tactics or strategies that male legislators employ that you feel that you can't employ?*
> A: Yes. And I can't explain what it is, but they have a—*they are stronger.* Maybe it is just me, but sometimes *I am afraid to make the decisions* . . . but they don't seem to be. I think they can see further ahead than a woman can in a way.

Q: *Well, conversely, do you think there are any particular tactics or strategies that you can employ that are not available to men?*
A: I think *we have the emotional*—I think we have the common sense more than a man has.

If you put people in terms of who contributed most it would be the economists who could see the total picture. They could contribute much more than *I*, who *could only bring out the idealistic* issues.

The Housewife-Benchwarmer, like the Spectator, occupies a position on the outer edges of the substantive legislative process.[10]

In a debate upstairs they have such qualified people . . . very little necessity [for me] to get up and speak. . . . [talking about work on committee] can never say that on the ladder of success my contribution was substantial.

I'll only speak on things which I'm knowledgeable about or . . . can really contribute to the passage or defeat of an issue. There haven't been that many things that I've been that knowledgeable about.

I am not that far out into things. I don't feel that I am . . . getting in there and plugging for this and for that. . . . All I want to do is to be able to sit here and have my vote and represent my people.

The Housewife-Benchwarmer generally will not get "that far out into things," because she feels herself to be inadequate compared to her colleagues. Her self-deprecating responses to the question, "Have you ever had any hesitancy about revealing your intellectual equality or superiority to men?" provide further proof that she feels inadequate.

[laugh] I don't really have to worry too much about that. No, not being particularly bright in the beginning I haven't ever had to hide any intellectual achievements.

God! I'm not that smart—so I haven't got any [hesitancy].

Well, I have never felt I was—so I can't say. No, I wouldn't hesitate if I really was superior.

She abhors all the bargaining and compromising she sees about her—"Being a politician isn't really my cup of tea"—but she does not feel sufficiently confident about herself and her ideas to confront her male colleagues with another style of operation. Consequently, under most circumstances the Housewife-Benchwarmer will take a back seat with regard to the policy-making process. She will probably function most effectively in casework for constituents.[11] "I think I have been most success-ful as a legislator helping my constituents in cases where they were not able to help themselves." This is the one area where she feels she can bring to bear her traditional feminine skills in interpersonal relationships with some degree of efficacy. How-ever, given the unusual conditions that prevail in the New Hampshire assembly, a Housewife-Benchwarmer may some-times find herself in an unexpected position. A Housewife-Benchwarmer who is chairman of the Public Health and Wel-fare Committee remarks:

I have been astounded to find my place at the place that I am. Each day I think I grow a little bit more afraid and a little more wary of what we are doing. I have been asked to speak at several clubs—small ones, you know—and I never have because I am not sure about my speaking; but finally a women's group called me the other day, and I looked over the past two years of the laws that we had passed in the health field, and I made up my mind that after all I was in the position of knowing what we had passed and and what we were facing, and that it was time perhaps that I did go out and tell other people. [several questions later] I have reservations about taking this power responsibility of chair-man. You see, I'll be honest, *I think there are other people who are more capable than I.*

Not surprisingly, the Housewife-Benchwarmer is somewhat suspicious of the current women's movement; but her attitude, sometimes bordering on the hostile, is based on little actual information.

I don't think Women's Lib is the answer, if that is what you're getting at.

Q: *Why do you think that "Women's Lib" is not the answer?*

A: Well, I think that it is a little far out. I think they are going to extremes.

Q: *Could you give me a specific example?*

A: No. Because I don't know enough about it. Because I don't want to know anything. I think they are all wrong.

Q: *What don't you go along with?*

A: Well, I can't remember what all the things are, but some of the things seem a little far out and really unnecessary.

Q: *What kinds of things seem unnecessary?*

A: I can't think of any of them right this minute. Can you tell me some and maybe I'll remember what they were?

Q: *Have you ever felt hindered because you were a woman?*

A: No. I really haven't, and that's why this feminist movement has surprised me a little bit. It seems as though it came up all of a sudden, and so many went to extremes, in my estimation. . . . I think they are doing themselves out of some of the privileges they had before.

Q: *How do you feel about the women's movement today?*

A: Yeach!

Q. *What don't you like about it?*

A: It is altogether too forceful. I think they are weakening their own position. I really do. I think they are losing the respect of men. . . . If a woman wants to make it in the political world, she can without going through this Women's Lib bit.

Q: *Is there anything you like about it?*

A: Sorry.

With her attitude toward the women's movement and her lack of information about its goals, and with her uncritical acceptance of women's present role in society, the Housewife-Benchwarmer lacks the motivation to represent the interests of women. In response to an open-ended question concerning their conception of their legislative role, none of these women mentioned the representation of women's interests as part of their job. When questioned further as to whether they were particularly concerned about representing the interests of women, they generally responded no.

Traditional Civic Worker

The Traditional Civic Worker is more common in Connecticut than in New Hampshire. Five out of the 10 women interviewed in Connecticut were so classified (2 senators and 3 assemblywomen), as compared to 4 out of 12 in New Hampshire (3 assemblywomen and the only senator who was interviewed). The Traditional Civic Worker has a positive self-image and a basically positive attitude toward women's present role in society, but she can be receptive to some change. In contrast to the remarkable uniformity displayed among the Housewife-Benchwarmers, Traditional Civic Workers display a degree of variation in their attitude toward women's role in society. This is probably related to differences in socioeconomic background. Whereas only one of the Housewife-Benchwarmers had a college degree, only two of the Traditional Civic Workers had no education beyond high school, and three had graduate degrees.[12] The Traditional Civic Worker also tends to have a higher family income than the Housewife-Benchwarmer. Her class background is likely to expose her to contemporary ideas, and her positive view of herself makes her unlikely to react passively to her environment. The net effect of her class and her self-image is to make her relatively articulate about her position as a woman and the overall position of women in society. She may incorporate some of the relatively "safe" ideas (those that appear to be innocuous) of the women's movement into her own world view, but she will adopt nothing that might lead her to question her basic life-style, which in terms of commitment to children and family life does not differ appreciably from that of the Housewife-Benchwarmer.

The Traditional Civic Worker's candidacy for the legislature involves a conscious decision. Although the initial idea may actually have been suggested by a husband, friend, or party official, the decision is hers and she does not feel herself to be the victim of ineluctable forces, as is often the case with the Housewife-Benchwarmer.

> We [the legislator and her husband] felt that the three running from our town were not strong on a broad-base tax . . . *we decided,* on talking it over, *Why don't I run?*

> I had been very active in local _____politics. . . . I figured the action was at the state level. *I saw the opportunity* to get elected. I didn't discuss the nomination with anyone.

> I was on the Board of Education at the time and extremely interested in the problems of education, and it was suggested that perhaps if I ran for a state office I could continue on a broader base in that area. . . .
> Q: *What were some of the pros and cons as you saw it then?*
> A: The pros were probably somewhat of a feeling of party responsibility . . . I felt a certain degree of loyalty. Also, *the excitement, the challenge* of being able to continue on in the educational field on a broader base . . . at this stage of the game all *our children have now married, and I have available time.*

> There were other men who wanted the nomination badly . . . my party chairman chose me . . . I was elated . . . I said I would have to ask my husband's permission before I allow you to use my name as a nominee.

> Q: *What were some of the pros and cons about running at that time?*
> A: *Some of the pros* . . . I have always wanted to do

something beyond being a housewife. I have a bachelor's
degree from Smith and a master's degree from Yale . . .
and I did all sorts of things like Red Cross Home Service,
etc. . . . I served on the Board of Education, and when I
dropped out of that I looked for something else to do. And
by that time I had become interested in government and
politics—it is really government that I am interested in, not
politics . . . *somebody has to be in that group that is making decisions to tell them what to do—and I intend to be
one of those.*

This legislator later decided to challenge the incumbent of the
senate seat she now holds: "I don't want to be egotistical, but I
have a certain amount of ability and it wasn't being touched
down there." As these responses indicate, the Traditional Civic
Worker is generally enthusiastic about the prospect of running
for the legislature, because she is confident about herself and
her abilities. She runs because she has been heavily involved in
substantive issues in her community and sees the legislative job
as an opportunity to continue in such activities. In effect the
Traditional Civic Worker is simply carrying out her self-as-
signed, public-service volunteer role in the legislature. Her commitment, then, is not to the game of politics per se but to the
broader issues of government. Whatever political ambitions she
has are a function of this commitment and her commitment to
her family roles. Her motivation to run for the legislature
derives from her concern with issues and a favorable family situation (children grown or a husband very supportive emo-
tionally and financially). This motivation, in combination with
her positive feelings about herself, enables her to face whatever
competition she has for the nomination. (Five of the Traditional
Civic Workers had opposition for their current seats.) Since the
basic motivating force for the Traditional Civic Worker is not
the status of political office but the desire to be effective with
regard to issues, she has progressive political ambitions only if
she feels that she can be more effective in a higher office and if
she feels that her family situation allows for such ambitions.

Q: *What about any other office?*
A: No. No, I have all I can handle with this. I might like
to run for the senate, but that is too much of a job . . . involves more hours than I can give to it . . . it's a matter of
time and my family . . . if you have seen some of the senators, I think *I can match up* to some of them; I don't think
that would be any problem.

I don't envision higher office. . . . . I don't like Washington.
The *action is on the state level.* I see no advantage in running for the senate. I can be governor, but I'm not interested in money matters: therefore I'm not interested in
being governor. Looking at my interests and my abilities, I
have as much here as any other place I can think of.

That was asked me some years ago when I was the only
woman in the senate. . . . I said, *"Nowhere,"* because *I am
service-minded.* I'm not concerned with whether I have a
title or not.

Where would you go from here? Congress? . . . it takes a
lot of money, and I don't have it. . . . I would hate to take
the kid out of school, and that has held me back in a way
. . . if I had the money, maybe the family would get caught
up in the idea.

Unlike the Housewife-Benchwarmer, the Traditional Civic
Worker's political ambitions are not limited by self-image, for
she does not doubt her capacity to handle greater responsibilities. An important limiting condition for many a Traditional
Civic Worker is something which was touched upon earlier—
age. Generally she is active in community volunteer work when
her children are young and moves into elective office only when
they are grown. Beginning her political career at a relatively advanced age necessarily limits her opportunities.[13] For example,
in the Eighty-fifth Congress, elected in 1956, the largest single
block of U.S. representatives first entered the House between
the ages of thirty-five and forty.[14] The one Traditional Civic
Worker who was motivated by an intense sense of civic duty

and was somewhat interested in running for Congress was over sixty-five years of age. For the Housewife-Benchwarmer political ambitions can be predicted with considerable accuracy: generally there are none. In the case of the Traditional Civic Worker the matter is considerably more complex, for her ambitions are a response to perceived opportunities: what family responsibilities allow, her assessment of where she can deal most effectively with the issues that concern her, and the political situation. Schlesinger's theory of political ambition would explain the lack of ambition among women as a realistic response to the political opportunities open to them.

With her positive self-image and her interest in specific issues, the Traditional Civic Worker becomes actively involved in the substantive legislative process once she enters the legislature. A Traditional Civic Worker in the New Hampshire assembly, who was one of the first freshman legislators ever assigned to the Judiciary Committee, explained that the chairman of the committee had asked her to sign up: "He sought me out because I was talented." This legislator was rather voluble during the interview about "my bills." Several of the Traditional Civic Workers went on at great length about the specifics of bills they had worked on. In this respect the Traditional Civic Worker is like Barber's "Lawmaker" type, who "continually turned the discussion in the direction of specific pieces of legislation . . . one of the most frequent nouns encountered in the Lawmaker's transcript is 'bill.' " [15] The responses of two Traditional Civic Workers to the question, "How do you think you have done so far as a legislator?" further illustrates this similarity:

> I'm satisfied with what I have done as a freshman. . . . I have been fortunate enough to get three or four bills passed, which I think is pretty good.

> I hope I have done a good job. I sponsored a piece of legislation last session which I got through despite the Commissioner of Motor Vehicles and a few other people [long, detailed discussion of how she developed the bill followed].

And like the Lawmaker the Traditional Civic Worker is especially concerned with producing and acting constructively. Satisfaction is derived from following through and finishing legislative tasks.[16]

> Q: *How would you describe the job of being a legislator?*
> A: Well . . . I really do think when you take a job you
> should be where the action of the job is. Probably the most
> important thing that you do is to *decide that there are im-
> portant things and then try to pursue them.*

> Q: *How do you think you have done so far as a legislator?*
> A: It has been a very rewarding experience for me. . . . I
> put in a great amount of time, and I am *very conscientious
> in following up my obligations* to individual constituents,
> and I am always available for speaking engagements and
> consultations. . . . My attendance record is excellent be-
> cause I have the time to do it. I would rather perform this
> way than go out after publicity . . . which is essential up to
> a point, but I function much better in the role of being able
> to do the work that I want to do in a careful, conscientious
> way.

> Q: *How would you describe the job of being a legislator?*
> A: I would describe it as being consumingly interesting,
> *actually being at the hub of where the wheels are going
> around.* . . . The most important thing is getting into an
> area which is important—like education is my specialty—
> and becoming an expert and being able to influence deci-
> sions in the way you think they should go.

> I come all the time. I work very hard and *look into every-
> thing* and speak when I want to, and I'm not afraid of any-
> one.

As these responses indicate, the Traditional Civic Worker is
extremely conscientious about her legislative duties and is generally willing to assert herself with regard to issues that concern
her. "I'm not an iffy person." "If I know I want something, I tell

it." Unlike the Housewife-Benchwarmer, who was hesitant about speaking on the floor, the Traditional Civic Worker will speak to issues on the floor "just as often as necessary" and is generally at ease when doing so. But she is sufficiently socialized to legislative norms to know that by speaking on all issues one may impair one's effectiveness. She also may have adopted some of the norms with regard to legislative bargaining. One such Traditional Civic Worker said, "Women can compromise as well as men and do—I do." A Traditional Civic Worker in Connecticut, who was bothered by the militancy of "the Women's Liberation" with regard to protective labor legislation, kept on stressing that "all those types of things are negotiable." Another Traditional Civic Worker had reluctantly come to accept bargaining as a necessary device for achieving her legislative aims:

> Q: *Have there been any other things that have given you problems?*
> A: Well, quite frankly I don't like the political bargaining, but this is part of the game, and you have to do this as a . . . legislator. . . . . . I wish I didn't have to bargain, but I find this is the way to get a bill through.

But the following incident suggests what can happen to the Traditional Civic Worker when she assumes a role whose demands may conflict with her central purpose—the pursuit of issues in the public interest. (The Traditional Civic Worker rarely talks about her district or her constituents; much more frequent are references to "the people" or "the public.")

> I was assistant leader in the senate in my third term here. . . . I offered myself as a candidate. I said I would like the job. . . . I was elected by my colleagues, and I never hated any job more. You have to be part of the team, and I am not that way [stated in a rather emphatic tone]. I am independent, and you have to work for and defend the party position. I knew this theoretically, but it was brought in on me. You can't stand up there on the floor and go against your

leaders. If you are the assistant to the minority leader you can't take a different position on the floor—well, you could, but even I, as independent as I am, saw that that isn't the way to play the game.

On the other hand, we are reminded once again of the difficulty of generalizing from a small sample by the fact that the Traditional Civic Worker in the New Hampshire senate was the assistant minority leader, and two of the Traditional Civic Workers in Connecticut were assistant leaders for their parties. The Traditional Civic Worker may come to accept bargaining as necessary, given the present array of interests in the legislature, but she does not particularly value the bargaining process as such. No Traditional Civic Worker expounded on the virtues of bargaining as a mechanism for discovering what is best for the public.

Basically accepting women's present role in society, the typical Traditional Civic Worker is not especially conscious of the salience of sex roles in the legislature. One of these legislators continually emphasized that she was treated "as one of the boys." In response to a question about whether women faced special problems when campaigning, this woman responded, "No, absolutely not—what problems could we face that are different from men?" Another Traditional Civic Worker commented, "No, there is nothing that we can't do that the men can do." But since the Traditional Civic Worker is actively involved in the legislature, she interacts more frequently with her male colleagues than does the Housewife-Benchwarmer (in New Hampshire it was apparent that many of the latter chose to "hang together" rather than "hang separately"); therefore she may become sensitive to having to "prove" herself because she is a woman, whereas her male colleagues are simply assumed to be competent. Half of the Traditional Civic Workers felt they personally had experienced this in their initial encounters in the legislature. Unlike the Housewife-Benchwarmer, the Traditional Civic Worker is active enough in the legislature to feel that she can legitimately compare herself to her male colleagues; she herself has no doubts about her abilities but notes that her male colleagues do not automatically accept what she knows to be true about herself. She is not,however, particularly indignant about the necessity to prove herself. She simply notes its existence, does what is required of her because of this expectation, and goes about her legislative business. "But I will have this to say: it is not hard once you say two or three intelligent things in committee—they accept you right away. It's not hard that way." Her male colleagues may very well accept her after she goes through this special "initiation rite"; what is more certain is that the typical Traditional Civic Worker accepts this inequality with little or no objection. Her solution to this problem is an individual one, as is her solution to any other problem she experiences as a woman. For instance, although most of the Traditional Civic Workers (like the Housewife-Benchwarmers) were quite pleased with the courtesies granted them by their male colleagues, one was not at all pleased. She recounted that she told her colleagues:

> "Don't treat me as a woman—don't be polite." . . . Many times when we go out to dinner there will be twelve men and me, and they want to take my check and put it in and divide it up by the twelve men. I have said, "There are thirteen senators here: divide it by thirteen, and let me pay my own way." Little ways like that I have had to fight, but they've accepted that now.

This incident indicates that the Traditional Civic Worker may in certain instances object when she feels that she personally is the recipient of unequal treatment, but with her basically positive feelings about herself and her accomplishments— Q: *"Why do you think you have been so successful as a legislator?"* A: "Because I'm right."—she is not interested in generalizing and comparing her experiences with those of other women. "I don't see why they [women] allow themselves to be held back." "I don't have this great Women's Lib feeling myself. . . . I've never seen the great barrier that other people see and feel is there; it's been invisible as far as I was concerned."

A preference for individual solutions and the basic acceptance of traditional sex roles is further illustrated by the Traditional Civic Worker's reaction to the exclusion of women from the "Hawaiian Room" in the capitol building in Connecticut. Her reaction is essentially the same as that of the Housewife-Benchwarmer: the men have the Hawaiian Room, and the women have the O.W.L.'s room—the latter being a ladies' lounge with some comfortable chairs and do-it-yourself cooking facilities. A Traditional Civic Worker observes:

> . . . this is the Hawaiian Room, that is the men's what you might call "lounge," and they have *very wild lunches* . . . and they have a lot of drinking . . . and women legislators are not members and can't be members. And there is a big fight around here because some of the women press want admittance.
> Q: *How do you feel about it?*
> A: I feel it is perfectly all right for the men to have their men's place if they want to.

A Housewife-Benchwarmer concurs:

> . . . the Hawaiian Room, which is the men's counterpart to the O.W.L.'s room . . . and the ladies can go anytime they are invited. But they are usually escorted there. And that's all right. We had this little newsgal that tried to get in last year, and she's taking it to court.

Clearly women's issues (at least the women's rights issues with which contemporary feminists are concerned) seldom have a high priority for the issue-oriented Traditional Civic Worker. In response to the question about their feeling any particular responsibility to represent the interests of women, several of the Traditional Civic Workers responded, "Not particularly." However, none responded with a flat no, as was often the case with the Housewife-Benchwarmer. If the Traditional Civic Worker said no, she always elaborated on her response:

> No. I feel if I represent my town and *represent what I think is good government,* I am representing women as well as

men. In some areas it can be a particular thing that per-
tained more to women—child care or something like this,
but I *really don't feel any connection* to one or the other.

No. But I am particularly concerned about representing
and presenting bills that women are more interested in—
housing, drugs . . .

The Traditional Civic Worker generally will not work in opposition to the issues being pushed by contemporary feminists (the
abortion issue is an exception). She may offer her support on
some issues, but it is a tempered support, and she will certainly
not place herself in the forefront of the battle.

Not any more than all interests. I am interested in women
and equality, and I will vote for the amendment that grants
equal rights to women, but not Women's Lib. *In fact I
rather like it the way it is.* I enjoy a man holding the door
open for me, and I enjoy being taken out to dinner occasionally. I like the preferential treatment a woman gets.
. . . On the other hand I feel very strongly that if a woman
is doing the equivalent of what a man is doing in industry
or the executive level, she should certainly be paid equally.

No, not particularly. I have fought for such things as the
Equal Rights Amendment that's before the Congress because I think it's fair and proper . . . but no, I have *never
identified myself, maybe that is one reason that I have had
as much success* as I do.

One Traditional Civic Worker used the question about concern
with women's issues to express her interest in seeing more
women in politics:

I am particularly interested in urging more women to come
into politics and community life.
Q: *Why?*
A: Because I think they have a great deal to add and
somewhat of a different point of view, frequently, from a
man's point of view, and I think practically *they have much*

more time available. . . . They do extremely well and very conscientiously. They are available for the day by day, hour by hour things.

This interest in seeing more women in politics, for the reasons articulated by this legislator, was universally held among the Traditional Civic Workers. They all responded enthusiastically to the question, "Are you particularly interested in seeing more women run for political office?" Some of the more interesting responses are noted below:

> Absolutely. *Women of higher quality and caliber are freer to get into public office than a man.* A lot of men with a lot of ability can't, but their wives could. Also, men with expertise could give this to their wives. Caliber of public officials would be higher just because the kind of man who is attracted to politics isn't successful in his business and private life. . . . Married women like myself, who are educated and have the financial advantage to be able to get into politics, are not doing it. I have friends across the country that would make excellent politicans, but they're . . . at home or they're head of the P.T.A. or head of some drive to collect funds. . . . There should be a difference in society's opinions of politicians; it's still the dirty, rotten, stupid politician image. I think we as women should be raising our sons and daughters to be politicians instead of doctors.

> Yes—because I think that perhaps most of them come from a background of voluntary service. . . . Women have a background of service to people, and I think this is terribly important if you go into politics. *They aren't as likely . . . to concentrate on where they personally are going to get—* more interested in where people are going to get because of what they do.

> Yes I am. . . . For one thing, they are *better than the run-of-the-mill male legislator.* . . . They are conscientious, hard-working—they are much harder for the political machine to push around. . . . *When a woman gets to run for*

representative, she has proven herself in her own district at home . . . whereas they will take almost any man for the nomination—a smart young lawyer—but a woman has to really prove it.

All of these legislators are suggesting that women should modify their traditional roles somewhat by entering public office. But it is also clear that the Traditional Civic Worker envisions no basic change in the division of labor between the sexes, for the advantages to be reaped by having more women in public office can be realized only if the status quo is maintained. The attitude that women are morally superior beings who will be able to purify politics is also evidenced in their responses. These arguments offered by Traditional Civic Workers actually bear a striking resemblance to those put forth by the late-nineteenth-century women's suffragists, who argued that women should be given the vote because of the purifying effects it would have on politics, as opposed to the earlier women's-suffragists, who argued for the vote as a matter of justice.[17] The matter of the social and political consequences of women's holding legislative office will be discussed later in this chapter.

Women's Rights Advocate

The discussion of the Women's Rights Advocate is somewhat tentative, as only two legislators—one in the Connecticut assembly and one in the New Hampshire assembly—were so classified. I actually began to see the Women's Rights Advocate as a clear type only after comparing the transcripts from New Hampshire and Connecticut to those from New York—three of the legislators in New York being classified as Women's Rights Advocates on the basis of the available transcripts. The data base here obviously has some significant limitations, but the direction of the contemporary women's movement since these interviews—impressionistically observed—leads me to believe that the Women's Rights Advocate is a distinct role type and one likely to become more common.

The Women's Rights Advocate has a positive self-image and a negative attitude toward women's current role in society: that is to say, she is interested in seeing considerable change in that role. Her positive self-image is reflected in the decision to run for the legislature. A New York State senator describes the circumstances that led to her nomination:

> *I'd been thinking about running for office. I'm sure a lot of people always do.* I took a look at the new lines and thought to myself . . . it looked like a district that I thought a woman in fact could run in. I think we have to be realistic: there are still some areas that a woman would have a lot more difficulty running in than other areas. . . . I thought I had a chance. So, I began to talk to people about it. . . . I said, "I'm interested in running for this office."
> Q: *Could you describe your first talk that you had with a party official about your nomination?*
> A: Oh, I didn't talk to party officials. I ran against the party. . . . I like to think of myself as an insurgent.

A New York State senator, who attained her senate seat after having first served in the assembly, describes the circumstances leading to her move to the senate:

> The district was represented by the then senior Republican. . . . I had my own interest that developed to a point where I felt I had to . . . I wouldn't stand it any more: I felt I had to get out of there. I had to start articulating some of the problems in our state that I saw, and felt the best way to do that was to do that in the capacity of a candidate.

A New York assemblywoman:

> I had been on my predecessor's staff for many years. . . . *I carried the load, and everybody back home knew it* . . . but when the time came for them to select a successor they not only didn't even think of me, but when I suggested that I might become a candidate they positively discouraged me. So I ran in the primary and won. This was the fall of————. I had a baby that same fall.

The typical Women's Rights Advocate is self-confident and is therefore willing to assert herself with regard to matters that she deems important (the word "fight" is used more frequently by the Advocate than by any of the other types), and if she thinks running for a particular office is necessary to accomplish her aims she will face whatever needs to be faced. Three of the Advocates endured heavy primary battles in their efforts to gain the nomination, while the other two were given the nomination in districts thought to be hopeless, but waged very intensive campaigns and won. The motivation to wage battles stems not from a love of the fray—the Advocate in Connecticut who led the fight to obtain a leadership position for women in the assembly noted, "I don't like to fight, and fighting is a very big part of politics, you know"—but from a deep concern with issues in the public realm. In this respect the Advocate is like the Traditional Civic Worker. For both there is the basic concern with issues, and for both the motivation to seek public office derives from their involvement with issues in their communities. An Advocate in New York states, "I see politics as really an extension of community activities." She herself became interested in electoral politics after seeing the "political ramifications" of her work with community groups on legal matters. Another in Connecticut stressed that she had been centrally involved in public affairs for twenty years, whereas her involvement in politics was very recent. She noted, "My whole training ground has been in the League of Women Voters." Two other Advocates became involved in community issues through student government in high school. As one related it:

> The interest to run for office came much later. . . . The reason that it came was the final feeling that I had reached a point of working at high levels in the staff position and *not being able to really influence the course of things as much as I wanted to.* . . . I felt that eventually the only way to advance the kinds of concerns and interests that I had was to take a crack at running for office myself and try to promote those things as an elected official.

There is, however, an important difference between the Advocate and the Traditional Civic Worker. Both are committed to "public affairs," but the Civic Worker sees her role as that of volunteer, whereas the Advocate is devoted to a professional career. The Civic Worker, if she is financially advantaged, may devote considerable time and energy to her volunteer role, but her basic identity is not derived from it, and at no point does she make any long-term psychic commitment to politics. She generally listed her occupation as "housewife." The Advocate, however, derives a basic part of her identity from her public affairs activities and is generally willing to make such long-term commitments. She always listed as her occupation the professional job she held before entering the legislature. One Advocate related the kinds of choices she felt she had to make in order to pursue her career:

I met my husband when we were both doing about the same work here. He's an attorney also and was a staff counsel to the speaker. . . . *I think almost all my life as far as my career was concerned I had long-range objectives.* I enjoyed my association with the men that I dated in those days, but I think as many women find *you reach the crucial point at which you have to make a decision if the individuals don't seem to be as concerned about your career objectives as they are about their own.* That always became the point at which we parted. . . . I don't think I ever would have married at all had I not been able to meet the kind of individual that I did . . . it works out fine because I was what I am when he married me, and he knew what the situation was, and that was part of the contract.

This kind of problem is never experienced by the Civic Worker, because she is committed to the traditional division of labor between the sexes. Whatever public affairs roles she assumes are strictly an adjunct to her family roles. Her situation is in a way structurally similar to that of males in this society who have "no basic choice as to whether or not to work. That a man will spend at least one third of his adult life in gainful work is a premise on which the plans of his life are based." [18] Likewise, the Civic Worker does not generally question whether or not to assume family roles; her choices are with regard to what kinds of volunteer roles she can or cannot assume. The Advocate, however, does confront such choices because of her career commitments. Whereas all the Civic Workers were married and had children, three of the five Advocates were married, and of these only two had children. All of the Advocates had professional careers before entering the legislature.

This difference between the Civic Worker and the Advocate in their commitment to family roles and public affairs roles has important implications for their political ambitions. For the Advocate family roles are important, but they do not hold the primacy they do for the Civic Worker; while most of the latter stressed the importance of a young mother's being home with her children, no Advocate ever did. Because of her less exclusive commitment to family roles the Advocate typically enters elective office at an earlier age than the Civic Worker. Thus age usually is not a limiting factor for her, and this long-term commitment to nonfamilial roles is in itself likely to contribute to progressive political ambitions. Another factor is the Advocate's likely reaction to the opportunities afforded women by the current political situation. It was suggested earlier that lack of political ambition among women may be a realistic response to the range of opportunities open; the Advocate, however, is interested in change and probably would not accept this situation with equanimity. And she will probably have links to women's activist groups outside the legislature which can provide the emotional and organizational support she would need in any attempts to change the opportunity structure. The three Women's Rights Advocates in New York had all been aided in their campaigns by the Women's Political Caucus.

The responses of the Advocates who were probed on their political ambitions contrast markedly with those of the typical Civic Worker. [19] A young, unmarried Advocate in New Hampshire:

I plan to be in it for quite a while. I would hope that I would run for the state senate. Then I have real high aspirations that I even might some day be down in Washington as our representative. *I'm looking for a bright future* in it.

A Women's Rights Advocate in New York:

I am going to—until I probably drop from exhaustion or something—*stay in this business* and keep working at it. . . . For me public service is a continuing goal whether it's staying in the senate or moving to some other office. I really don't know at this point. I have been approached to think about being on the state ticket in the Democratic party next year. I just haven't made up my mind. . . . As with all my decisions that I've made, career-wise, it will be a decision based on whether I can . . . be more effective in that next role.

As with the Civic Worker, the Advocate's positive self-image and concern with issues lead her to become an active participant in the substantive legislative process. The Advocate likewise talks freely about her accomplishments and her policy concerns, but because she does not share the Civic Worker's positive attitude toward women's present role in society she develops different substantive interests and makes different sorts of demands on her male colleagues. The Advocate is not at all content with women's roles; in fact she would like to see considerable change in it.

Women occupy a very second-class status in this society, and I think it's just time that ended.

So, it's that kind of thing, to really accept us as equals. But if we were accepted as equals there [political parties] I think that would be an example of the fact that we were accepted as equals in other places in society, and we're not.

I do think the role of women in society does have to be upgraded drastically.

Discontented with women's opportunities, the Advocate comes to give women's rights issues a special place in her value hierarchy. Although these are not her only areas of concern—the Advocates here are not exclusively identified with such issues, and every one of them had some expertise in the traditional feminine issue area of education—women's rights matters are not merely another policy concern. Women's rights was one of the factors that led to one Advocate's initial interest in politics. Another Advocate in New York, asked if she ever felt pressured to represent the interests of women, responded:

> No, *I have a natural feeling about this,* because I believe that the areas of discrimination are there, and they're serious ones. . . . I don't feel any enormous pressures because I've always been a part of it. Nobody had to drag me into the movement. . . . I have legislative responsibility in this area. I've had no pressure to do it; it's part of my own inclination.

An Advocate in Connecticut offered her advice to women just starting out in politics:

> You do have a special responsibility as a woman. . . . Looking at the whole thing and seeing how terribly hard it is to get here and get into any decent kind of position, remember that you are terribly fortunate, and make the most of it. *Do do things for them. Don't be up there as a woman*—and there are some of these—*and not do things for women. You do have a responsibility.*

Because the Advocate is acutely aware of the salience of sex roles—both in the legislature and in society at large—she does not merely respond to pleas for support from women's activist groups but assumes a leadership role in generating issues. She may work with such groups in developing legislation to improve the status of women, or she may lead organizational efforts within the legislature to enhance the power position of women legislators. Whereas the Traditional Civic Worker may observe certain disparities between the sexes but accept the situation with equanimity or at most attempt an individual solution, the Women's Rights Advocate is likely to react with righteous indignation and attempt collective solutions.[20] In contrast to the reactions of both the Housewife-Benchwarmers and Traditional Civic Workers, the Women's Rights Advocate in Connecticut could not readily accept the exclusion of females from the Hawaiian Room. She initiated the discussion of the situation herself:

> I do not like to be a woman in a capitol where the men eat their lunch in a separate room. . . . It is ridiculous that women have to sit in a separate room to eat lunch. . . . The very fact that you would have a room like that says something about attitudes which you are not even aware of. . . . The majority of [women] legislators . . . have not been aware that this is an exclusionary kind of thing . . . they don't feel that there is anything unusual about that; they are kind of glad to have their own room. . . . I find this very strange.

Similarly, the Advocate does not have the Civic Worker's mild reaction to the phenomenon of women having to prove themselves:

> I do think I have a certain amount of competence. . . . I've discovered that I know quite a lot more than a lot of those people. . . . If any man did some of the things that I have done . . . he would have had by now a much stronger position than I do. And I feel very, very, very strongly that again it is not me—it is not any one woman—because I have been involved now in bringing this issue out—it is simply the way things are. It is a very male society in here.

This legislator tried to organize around this issue for, although she herself might be capable of meeting the special demands placed on women—"In order to be equal you have to be so much better than anybody else in the world, and that is not equality"—she is intensely concerned about women as a class. The Civic Worker, feeling quite confident about her own abilities, simply meets the special requirements and tends to disassociate herself from other women. The Advocate is also confident about her own abilities; however, she derives satisfaction not only from demonstrating what she herself can do but also from working with other women to realize the collective strength of women. This Advocate describes her feelings about the effort to place a woman in a position of leadership within the Democratic party:

> It was a tremendous experience for all of us. We really pulled together. . . . I really felt there was an injustice somehow. . . . We put the energy in: therefore we ought to have a little more responsibility. . . . If we are not really effective up here, let's not pretend we are.
> Q: *Do you think that women are somewhat more effective since the caucus?*
> A: Definitely. Every one of us. First of all we're more self-confident. Secondly, we are all visible now, which we really weren't before. Thirdly, the men are aware that we are basically not far-out types. . . . We did try to get along all these years . . . and we will be asking for other things for women, definitely. And really it has strengthened every woman.

As these remarks indicate, the Advocate derives considerable gratification from awakening the consciousness of both her female and male colleagues. An Advocate in New York recalled an incident when the deputy majority leader was speaking on behalf of a particular bill and repeatedly said, "We need to get more qualified men." She reported:

> So with a smile I said, "Senator, would you yield to a question?" He said, "Yes," so I said, "Senator, would you just amend your remarks to say 'person' instead of 'man'? . . . I'd like you to change that to 'person' so that we could at least have the possibility of women on the Board of Regents. Maybe by raising our consciousness we'll consider having more women. . . ." Half the time these fellows

don't even realize that there are discriminations. But you raise the issue and you point it out to them, and they have to say, "Yes, you're probably right."

The Advocate is considerably more conscious of the salience of sex roles than any other of the role types discussed, and as hypothesized she also appears to experience considerably more conflict between traditional feminine role expectations and professional expectations. Whereas the other types primarily experience role conflict (if they perceive it at all) as a problem of allocating time between their different responsibilities, the Advocate is sensitive to the incompatible expectations of the roles she holds. She is insistent that she be accorded the full privileges and responsibilities normally associated with the role of legislator, and she will react with considerable indignation when she feels she has not received equitable treatment. However, the Advocate does not necessarily prefer all the behaviors normally associated with masculine roles to those associated with traditional feminine roles. Her personal role conception is one that includes some traditional feminine dispositions as well. Because of this personal conception, role-conflict resolution is not always as simple a matter as was originally hypothesized. The Advocate in Connecticut feels that women in politics are under unique pressures:

> You don't want to be active like a man in a society like this. You don't want to lose that something which does make you a woman. You don't want to become so aggressive and so hard that you lose something else in the process. . . . You have to watch that you don't harden too much.

An Advocate in New York sees "the issue of whether it's an appropriate role" as the major problem that women in politics have had to face. She sees herself as "constantly fighting the battle of proving that we're still women and still feminine, and having a brain and wanting to have a career is not mutually exclusive with being a woman."

Although the Advocate may be frustrated with the limitations

of the traditional feminine role, she is by no means totally disaf-
fected with it—and so in a conflict situation will not always opt
for the professional role. Her response is dependent on the degree to which she values the particular feminine role expectation: if it is an expectation she values, she may favor the feminine role (for instance, empathy is more likely to be valued than
passivity). It is also possible that there will be a disparity between her role disposition and her role behavior. The structural
demands of the legislature and her assertive personality impel
her toward assuming the professional role, but this behavior will
not necessarily coincide with her personal disposition, which is
more nearly related to her underlying values and self-identity.
The matter is in need of further exploration, but the data do appear to suggest that, although behaviorally the Women's Rights
Advocate appears to adopt the nonfeminine role frequently, she
is also sensitive to the dilemma posed by Virginia Woolf in *Three
Guineas*—that women in their effort to become what they might
be in a free world might lose the best of what they are now.

Passive Women's Rights Advocate

The discussion of the Passive Women's Rights Advocate will
necessarily be very brief—because of all the women interviewed
only two, both first-term legislators in the Connecticut assembly, were so classified. Admittedly it is risky, if not impossible, to generalize on the basis of only two cases, but I believe it
is important to discuss why these two women do not fit into the
other categories. The Passive Women's Rights Advocate has a
negative self-image and a negative attitude toward women's role
in society. As stated earlier, I had originally hypothesized that
this category would be blank, on the ground that individuals
with these attributes would be so overcome with negativism
that they would not be able to take such a decisive action as
running for political office. Barber, however, suggests that some
individuals with low levels of self-esteem may run for office out
of a need to obtain or confirm a higher self-esteem. "Political office-holding can offer some strong and specific rewards to the

damaged self." [21] A political office may be appealing to a woman who has doubts about her abilities but believes that women should assume more active roles in society. Running for elective office may provide a vehicle for a positive assertion of her self and individuality (neither of these women had a professional career; both were in their mid-fifties and had grown children). Each of the Passive Women's Rights Advocates became a candidate upon the urging of others: "They started working on me to take her place—" "It became more insistent on the part of the women urging me to run." They do not approach political office with the fear and trepidation of the Housewife-Benchwarmer, but neither do they share the self-confidence of the Traditional Civic Worker and the Women's Rights Advocate. They are simply "interested." This interest can be realized in a place like Connecticut, where competition for the state assembly in many districts is relatively undemanding of a candidate's resources. The Passive Advocate does not continually point to her accomplishments—"I am not satisfied with what I have been able to accomplish; I really haven't passed any bills under my own name. . . . I probably didn't have the kind of bright ideas that are needed"—but neither does she react passively to the legislative environment, for like the Advocate she is concerned about legislative practices which reflect society's valuation of women. Both of the Passive Advocates expressed considerable displeasure with the Hawaiian Room, for example, and wanted to see more women in leadership positions. She also is intensely interested in measures to improve the status of women: "Why should women have less input into the real control and direction our society is going in?" However, lacking the Advocate's self-confidence, she will generally not exercise leadership in these areas. It is difficult to speculate about how common the Passive Advocate is: the growth of the current women's movement and the fact that the two Passive Advocates were found in Connecticut, where the activities of women's activist groups in the state had a visible impact on the activities of the legislature (role conceptions of individual legislators and the development of issues), suggests that Passive Advocates will become more common as the ideas of the movement become more accepted and the organizational efforts of feminist groups more developed. However, the tendency of established institutions to incorporate only those ideas which do not demand significant alteration of current practices, and the increasing professionalization of state legislatures, suggest that middle-aged housewives without professional careers are not likely to fare well in political office, whatever their ideological convictions may be.

The fourfold typology of female legislators emerged from the attempt to understand individual legislators, to explore the contents of their sociopsychological world and their mode of adaptation to it. Beyond this lies the question of the functional significance of the tasks these women perform. *What functions do women serve in state legislatures?* Here the focus shifts to the institutions themselves. The Connecticut and New Hampshire assemblies provide the rare opportunity to study the functional implications of female behavior in a nonfamilial male-dominated institution.

The literature on the interaction processes of goal-oriented groups has posited that the maintenance of such groups is dependent on the development of a system of role differentiation. Certain actors assume the task-leader or instrumental roles and others assume the supportive or emotional-expressive roles.[22] Within the nuclear family the father generally assumes the instrumental role, the mother the emotional-expressive role.[23] If we assume that these are meaningful categories, clearly at least some males perform this necessary emotional-expressive function in most state legislatures (Barber suggests that the Spectator's main contribution to the legislature is that of reducing tension),[24] simply because there are not enough women to perform it. What happens when there are enough women? Do women legislators take on their "natural" functions, thereby relieving those men who have done special duty?

The previous discussion should have made clear that it is difficult, and perhaps meaningless, to discuss the role behavior of *the* female legislator. The Housewife-Benchwarmer, given her passive role orientation and admiration of traditional feminine values and behaviors, very likely does perform the emotional-expressive function. A Housewife-Benchwarmer in Connecticut remarks: "I have tried to build up the ego in some people rather than to tear it down. I have done that on occasion, taking the backside and let him bring it forward if he has done his homework . . . there is a man here I wanted to help quite a bit along those lines." The Housewife-Benchwarmer, because of her felt inadequacies, is somewhat in awe of the legislature—"upstairs they have such qualified people"—and thus contributes to an atmosphere of prestige, effectively providing a supportive working environment for legislators who are more actively engaged in formulating policy.

The Traditional Civic Worker is basically task-oriented. Does this mean that she becomes a task leader? Does she still perform the emotional-expressive function? If task leadership is defined as occupying an officially designated leadership position, then very few of the female legislators are task leaders in New Hampshire, and even fewer in Connecticut. But if task leadership is defined in terms of the indispensable nature of a member's contributions, then the situation is not as clear. "Insofar as any member's contributions are particularly indispensable, they may be regarded as leaderlike; and insofar as any member is recognized by others as a dependable source of such contributions he is leaderlike." [25] A Traditional Civic Worker in Connecticut expressed a similar notion when asked if women held leadership positions:

Not as such, but I don't think that the fact of a title to leadership necessarily has anything to do with leadership . . . I don't believe that people who lead this legislature are in so-called leadership positions. You don't lead people out on the floor; you lead them in here, and there's many a woman who has influence in her committee or in her contacts with men around here. I think women very often set up a kind of standard that brings out the best in people, by their behavior and their industry and devotion to things they believe in.

A male colleague of this legislator remarked, "_____ does not do a lot of unnecessary talking in caucus, but when she talks, we listen." This Civic Worker could be classified as a "task leader," for she certainly facilitates task achievement by her dependability. As detailed earlier, the Civic Worker typically derives her satisfaction from the completion of tasks; therefore, if her colleagues come to rely on her knowledge and her ability to follow through on legislative tasks, she may function as a task leader. But although Civic Workers may function in this way (particularly in legislatures where the family-breadwinner role makes it difficult for many male legislators to be dependable task facilitators), this role does not appear to preclude their functioning in emotional-expressive (or "social-emotional") roles. This same Civic Worker comments:

> The thing that motivates my behavior here is that I honestly don't believe that under any circumstances you ought to belittle the other fellow. . . . I would feel badly if I would even though it might be a means to an end . . . you're more likely to get where you want to go if in the getting you don't step on other people or take away from them.

Given that the Civic Worker is primarily motivated by the advancement of particular issues rather than the advancement of her own political career and basically accepts many of the traditional expectations associated with the feminine role, it is not surprising that she can also facilitate tension-free interpersonal relationships. It was noted earlier that female legislators are often self-conscious about behavior which might appear to be self-promoting. The Civic Worker, pursuing her legislative interests in her selfless public-service fashion, can both contribute to a lessening of interpersonal hostilities—thereby helping to maintain the legislature as an institution—and attend to the more goal-oriented or instrumental needs of the legislature. (One female legislator in Connecticut did remark that some male legislators referred to certain women as "pain-in-the-neck do-gooders.") Not primarily concerned with credit for herself, she may let others receive public recognition if that will speed the completion of legislative work.

The Women's Rights Advocate is similarly task-oriented and so may also function as an informal task leader. Her career orientation, however, makes her less likely to allow others to take credit for her accomplishments. In fact, the Advocate may very well contribute to an increase in the tension level of the legislature. An Advocate in New York remarks: "I think a lot of people didn't know how to deal with the women coming in this year . . . I think they think they have to react a little differently or change a little bit . . . that puts them in a very uptight position." These male legislators may simply be reacting to "the fact that women are now part of the legislature," but the majority of the new female legislators in New York are also Women's Rights Advocates. Her style and the kinds of demands the Advocate is likely to make on her male colleagues will undoubtedly raise anxieties, thereby increasing interpersonal tensions. A legislator in Connecticut noted: "The men in the house . . . are really terrified of women because they know that they are getting together and getting organized." Although the data do not permit a careful examination of the reactions of male legislators. I suspect that male legislators—no matter how sympathetic they might be to the goals of the women's movement—must experience some degree of strain in interactions with Advocates simply because the Advocate is concerned with change, and change, even if desired, involves strain. The reflections of a Civic Worker in New Hampshire as to why she feels that, as a woman, she "can get around things just a little bit more than a man" provide some confirmation of this hypothesis:

> You know, I got married to have final decisions made by my husband, not me. And they [male colleagues] sit there and are shocked. . . . Women don't do these things nowadays. They want to run the house and run the men and run this and run that. . . . And they don't spank the kids . . . and I'll say I spank them, and they like that. That's good, you

know—that's more like the women were when I was
growing up . . . they seem surprised when I say something
like this, and *happy to think that there is a woman who
agrees with what they think.*

This Civic Worker does not cause her male colleagues much
discomfort, because she conforms to their expectations of
proper sex-role behavior. Because she fits into things as they
should be, it is quite likely that her sex status is less obtrusive
than that of the Advocate, who does not conform to the traditional expectations. Epstein has noted:

Often sex status intrudes less when it is permitted expres-
sion in normal sex-role behavior. For example, women who
work in tradition-bound law firms often find that male colleagues are used to treating women in a courtly manner
and can work best with women who are comfortable with
such treatment. Problems arise only where woman demand
they be treated "just like the men," causing their colleagues discomfort. Attempts to suppress sex-role behavior
in such contexts only succeed in making it obtrusive.[26]

The Advocate, who is ultimately concerned with making sex
status less relevant or irrelevant (in the allocation of roles and
responsibilities, both in the legislature and society at large),
probably causes all legislators—male and female—to be more
self-conscious about the extent to which their behavior is conditioned by their sex status. And such self-consciousness undoubtedly results in an increase of interpersonal tensions within
the legislature.

The extent to which women legislators function informally to
increase or decrease interpersonal tensions is largely determined by the personal role conceptions of individual legislators;
but the extent to which women legislators function as formal
task leaders is determined by the structural requirements of the
legislature. Women are better represented in formal leadership
posts in the New Hampshire assembly than in the Connecticut
assembly, not because of any particular aggressiveness on the

part of women in New Hampshire, but because of the basic
scarcity of talent within the institution itself, which forces the
male leadership to make use of the available female talent.
There is, however, one presumed female talent of which the
leadership in both assemblies is more than willing to avail itself.
"They like to make women clerks of committees . . . they can
associate women with being secretaries." "If there are six men
and two women on a committee, they'll look to women for
clerk." In Connecticut, where all the committees are joint
senate-house committees, six of the twenty clerks were women.
In the New Hampshire house women were the clerks in 11 of
the 22 committees.

The differences between the two assemblies in the assignment of women to formal task positions that allow the occupant
to formulate policy are striking. In Connecticut women did not
chair any of the standing committees. Each party had a woman
in one of the assistant leader positions, but these positions were
obtained only after considerable pressure by the women in each
party on their respective leaderships. In New Hampshire
women were chairpersons of 7 committees and vice-chairper-
sons of 3. As table 5.2 indicates, some of these women headed
very important committees in policy areas that are traditionally
regarded as nonfeminine.

Table 5.2 Leadership Positions Held by Women in the New Hampshire
House of Representatives, 1972

Chairman	*Vice-Chairman*
Education	Appropriations
Environment and Agriculture	Interstate Cooperation
Executive Departments and Administration	Judiciary
Interstate Cooperation	
Labor, Human Resources, and Rehabilitation	
Public Health and Welfare	
Ways and Means	

It appears that women were assigned to these important positions because of the "bankruptcy of talent" within the legislature. "You have a speaker who has had to rely on very capable

women because there haven't been that many capable men to spread around." There are few capable men around because the perquisites of legislative office in New Hampshire do not stir the ambitions of young men. The salary of $200 biennially makes it very unlikely that there will be a sufficient number of young men interested in seeking the large number of available seats. Retired persons ("who have nothing else to do") and women therefore become very common. The average age of the legislators serving during this session was sixty-seven. In this situation, described by one legislator as somewhat "weird"—where some legislators literally spend a considerable amount of time sleeping "on the floor" of the house—middle-aged women who have no outside occupations and have been active in their communities can be a valuable resource. It is also clear, however, that use of this resource is dependent on the personal predispositions of the leadership; there are no institutional mechanisms for the recognition of female talent. Most of the women legislators attributed the success of women in this session to the efforts of the current speaker, who was more willing than any previous speaker to put the talents of women to use.

> _____ is very good about putting women on as chairman or vice-chairman. He has one vice or one chairman and one vice . . . *it can't be two men or two women. Well, I guess it can be two men, but not two women.*

This legislator's remarks suggest the weight of the institutionalized norms that work against putting women into positions of leadership—even in a legislature where women have been relatively common for many years. One female legislator felt that previous speakers might have recognized the talent of women but not used it because they felt it would not be wise politically. The present speaker was described as "looking more at the good of the whole state." His motivations cannot be explored, but it is clear that he was bucking tradition and that he incurred some resentment, particularly from those men who lost their positions to women. Most of these women who were said to be more capable than the men they replaced had no specialized skills other than the willingness to pursue legislative work in a conscientious fashion, but such willingness appears to be a rare commodity in the New Hampshire assembly. A woman who chaired the Education Committee recounted:

> When I found out that I had won the primary, I sat down and I said, "_____, I don't know whether I am really capable of accepting this job and doing it if I'm elected." And I got kind of cold feet. But *after I got over here and found the caliber of the house* to be as it is, I feel that I have as much capability as the next person.

Personal role conceptions are clearly a function not only of the individual's personality but also of the conditions of work. A number of women who serve in middle-level leadership positions in New Hampshire probably would not fulfill the requirements of such roles in more professional legislatures.

In the Connecticut assembly it appears that few women hold leadership positions, not because they are less talented than the women in New Hampshire, but because the general level here is much higher. The decline in the number of seats as a consequence of reapportionment has generated increased competition for legislative seats, leading, as demonstrated earlier, to a decline in the number of women serving. "With reapportionment each seat becomes more important, and you fight more for it, and you can't indulge in the luxury of having a lot of women running." Younger men and lawyers are now more plentiful, and so the leadership has not had to turn to women. The average age of the male legislators serving in the 1965 session was 52, while since reapportionment in 1967 the average age has been 45. In 1965 12 percent of the legislators were lawyers; in 1967 the percentage jumped to 28 percent and has remained at about that level for each of the succeeding sessions. As I stated earlier, the women obtained their two leadership positions in this session only because of their own organizational efforts. There are many women in the Connecticut assembly with personal role conceptions that would permit them to occupy leadership positions comfortably; but very few of them do, because the institutionalized norms work against them. "I don't use that word very often, but it is a very male institution in here."

I now turn to the last question concerning sex roles. *What are the social and political consequences of allowing individuals to occupy both the status of female and the status of state legislator?* I have already touched on this question, but the primary focus here will be on the consequences of this situation for the policy output of the institution and for the overall status of women in society.

As chapter 4 indicated, the most visible social consequences of allowing a significant number of women to enter the legislature is that interactions between female and male legislators are mediated by the traditional courtesies that color interactions outside the legislature. Male legislators simply do not interact with female legislators as they would with legislators of their own sex. Women do not break into the "backslapping camaraderie." "I don't think they accept the women representatives as regular colleagues. I think they just put us in a different category." This special treatment may in some instances allow particular legislators to gain certain advantages, but these advantages are in the long run costly to women as a class, as each short-run gain reinforces the prevailing belief that women are not the equals of men.

There is also considerable social segregation by sex. Undoubtedly part of this is a consequence of feelings about propriety, but the courtesies demanded by female-male interactions may be experienced as a strain which interferes with effective communication. One legislator noted:

> I think just the fact that they have what looks like the smoke-filled political bosses' room, the exchange of ideas is a little easier. I'll give you an example. I happened to be here a little late the other night, and the men were discussing one of the bills, and there was disagreement amongst four or five of them, and of course almost immedi-

ately when the argument became heated they were hurling
invectives at one another, and then of course they realized
that I was sitting there, and they immediately stopped, and
yet I got some good ideas out of their discussing this bill
and what I call men's way of discussing.

This legislator felt that a consequence of social segregation is to
deprive women of a style of communication that leads to productive challenges. Though some women agreed that such
segregation deprives women of valuable information, this belief
was by no means unanimously held by the females in either
state. Many of the legislators felt that the exchange of information among the women at lunchtime was very fruitful. In New
Hampshire the women who chair committees generally lunch
together. Though one might suspect that social segregation
would tend to reinforce women's less-than-equal status within
the legislature, the data do not lead to any firm conclusions. But
the questionnaire data from New Hampshire do provide one interesting piece of information. Among the 14 women who
lunched with male legislators "frequently," 6 scored at the highest activity level, whereas among the 25 women who lunched
with male legislators less frequently only 1 scored at the highest
activity level.

The political consequences of having women in the legislature clearly depend on the particular women. Their personal
role conceptions determine the extent to which the interests of
women will actually be represented. The composition of the
New Hampshire house of representatives approximates the sex-
ual division in the electorate more closely than does the composition of any other state legislative body in the nation, but this
fact does not explain what the New Hampshire house does. In
her exhaustive analysis of the concept of representation, Hanna
Pitkin distinguishes between "descriptive representation," the
extent to which representatives reflect the social characteristics
of those they formally represent, and "representing as 'acting
for,' " the activity of representatives on behalf of or in the interest of others.[27] The data here indicate that "the substance or

content of acting for others" [28] is determined by the personal role conceptions of legislative representatives. Thus assessment of the political consequences of having female legislators involves examination of the variation in role conceptions in a particular legislature. Paul Peterson, in an examination of participation by the poor in community action programs, argues that in order to assess the character of substantive representation the representative's influence as well as his orientation must be considered. "The more influential the representative, the more effective his representation." [29] Hence the position from which a female legislator can act on her orientation is crucial. Though influence is not solely determined by orientation, it is clear that the orientation of the Housewife-Benchwarmer makes it impossible for her to achieve an influential position.

The discussion of role orientations showed that each role type is associated with a particular conception of what the interests of women are and a sense of obligation to those interests. It might be said that each role type is related to a different subjective evaluation of the interests of women. On the other hand, when I state that the extent to which the interests of women will be represented is determined by personal role conceptions, I am implying that the interests of women are an objective matter. The notion that women form a class and that the interests of this class are objectively determinable is a heavily debated issue in certain sections of the women's movement today. Here I will simply state that when I speak of "women's interests" I refer, not to education and welfare and such traditional female concerns, but to policies that seek to upgrade the status of women in society or to enable women to control their own lives more readily. Though such policies today are the expressed preferences of only some women, I believe that they are in the interests of all women. My belief is based on the proposition that if women were to experience the *results* of such policies they would *choose* such policies over the status quo. [30]

Assessment of the political consequences of the role conceptions held by female legislators in a given legislature is highly tentative: none of the legislatures was studied comprehensively, and there are no hard data on actual policy output or organizational activity outside the legislature. Some conclusions can be drawn, however. There appears to be little substantive representation of women's interests in the New Hampshire legislature—the typical female legislator here does not see herself as "acting for" women. The Housewife-Benchwarmer—so common because of the nonselectivity of the recruitment process—is pretty much incapable of "acting for" any interest. The Traditional Civic Worker can actually achieve some degree of influence, given the general level of competence in the house, but her values do not lead to an orientation conducive to "acting for" women. Because these two types predominate, the female legislators in New Hampshire do not operate together politically as women. One legislator recounted that several of the women had just met to "bat around ideas of some type of legislation that all the women could back." When asked if this occurred often she responded,

> They've never done this before, a report came back from a convention in Mobile that women legislators in other states had banded together to support and work on legislation that . . . would bring to light the importance of women in legislation; not necessarily women's liberation type legislation—probably more humane things.

It does seem ironic that in the legislature where women are the most numerous—"no other legislative body on earth has so many women members, never has had and probably never will"—the impetus for such an innovation should come from activities in other states.[31] Such ideas do not originate in New Hampshire because the personal role conceptions of the women representatives do not lead to innovative thinking with regard to the representation of women. Moreover, the organizational development of women's activist groups outside the legislature is so primitive that the legislators are under no pressure to modify their orientations. The state of this development strongly suggests that the favorable representation of women in the house since the 1930s has been of no consequence for the political development of women in New Hampshire. Nor has it had any effect on the overall direction of policy in New Hampshire—

a state not particularly well known for the humaneness of its policies.[32]

In both Connecticut and New York there appears to be considerably more activity with regard to the representation of women's interests. This apparent similarity exists despite the fact that there has never been more than a handful of women representatives in New York. In both states there is some "acting for" women among the women legislators. In New York the female legislators get together to jointly sponsor legislation dealing with women's issues. And as indicated earlier, women in Connecticut have attempted to organize in order to gain a share of power commensurate with their numbers. It is very difficult to assess the impact of this activity on "actual representation." A legislator in New York noted,

> We've not really succeeded very much with moving those bills, but I think the very fact that it took a couple of years to get one of the joint legislative committees to address themselves to the question of employment discrimination against women was a token response to our persistence.

In Connecticut the organizational unity achieved for the purpose of attaining positions for women does not maintain itself with regard to substantive issues. One legislator lamented that on many issues which came up "either no woman has spoken or maybe one." The few women who have attained formal positions of influence have orientations which preclude their vigorously "acting for" women. Probably they obtained their positions only because of their status quo orientations. In both states, however, the activity of the Women's Advocates in the legislature, in conjunction with the activity of women's activist groups outside the legislature, seems to have had some impact on the orientation of all legislators—female and male. Movement is not always in the direction of greater receptivity to change. There may be some backlash. But in both New York and Connecticut, organizational developments within and without the legislature have created the potential for the substantive representation of women.

6: Overview and Outlook

Before I review my findings and consider in this final chapter the questions raised, I would like to interject a personal note about the growth of my ideas from the time this project first began. Though it is difficult to recapture my exact feelings and thoughts—perhaps I am imagining that differences between then and now are greater than they actually are—I believe that my early ideas contained an unconscious bias. My initial hypotheses about the consequences of competition for office were derived from the belief that the forces of modernization were inexorably leading away from the differentiation of sex roles and toward the adoption of androgynous life styles. And though I used the term "androgynous," derived from the Greek roots *andro* (male) and *gyn* (female), my notion of what behavior would be like when sex roles were no longer relevant was based on masculine patterns. I imagined that both men and women would share in the task of childrearing, but beyond this my vision of equality was essentially the adoption by women of most of the values, attitudes, and behaviors of the prevailing culture. The norm of human behavior was male behavior. The question of whether sex roles are in fact changing is an empirical matter and can be answered only if the criteria for evaluation are sex-neutral. Whether or not change is socially desirable and whether the apparent direction of change is desirable are normative matters and must be treated separately. When unconscious biases such as I have described are present, there is a tendency for values to merge with the empirical assessment, and data that do not fit with the held values may even be lost, that is, patterns that are a mix of the feminine and masculine may simply go unnoticed. Or even worse, feminine or mixed

165

patterns may be labeled regressive or politically immature. Contemporary feminist scholars are discovering that this latter bias has been rife in political behavior research.[1] I now recognize the consequences of these biases and hope that my awareness has allowed me to see all that the data have to offer.

With respect to the consequences of seat competition for the sex composition of legislatures and the behavioral differences between female and male legislators, my original hypothesis was that competition would be inversely related to both the proportion of female legislators and the degree of sex-related differences. The first part of the hypothesis was confirmed by the aggregate analysis in chapter 2, but the survey data in chapter 3 indicated that the second part needed some revision.

Women are much less likely to be elected to the legislature in states where there are many potential competitors for a seat than in states where there are relatively few competitors. New Hampshire has the largest proportion of women legislators of any state, simply because it has more seats relative to its population than any other state. Cultural and political traditions were also discovered to be important for the contemporary pattern of female representation. And though the increased political activity by women in the early 1970s has led to an increase in the total number of women serving in state legislatures, the relative differences among the states has yet to change.

The survey of female and male legislators in the four New England states which historically have had the highest proportions of women legislators confirmed that women are more likely to be elected when the recruitment process is not very selective. The legislators in these states have quite varied backgrounds. They are generally not professional politicians; many first obtained their seats by being asked to run. Women are common, but retired persons are even more common. Women elected in competitive situations are likely to have more extensive political careers than men prior to entering the legislature. Their involvement may be even greater than that of men recruited under comparable circumstances, confirming that in the more competitive situation women may need to compensate for their "deficiencies." However, more competitive recruitment processes were found to accentuate rather than modify certain behavioral differences in the legislature itself. In general women were somewhat less likely to engage in assertive forms of activity and were more likely to be averse to legislative bargaining. These differences almost always increased among legislators who faced more competition for their seats and had more extensive political careers. It was suggested that these results may have been due to the basic nonselectivity of the recruitment process in these states: there was simply insufficient variation to test adequately the hypothesized relationship between competition and sex differentiation. These data still needed to be taken into account, and so it was proposed that the relationship between competition and sex differentiation was actually curvilinear. Where competition for office is minimal, sex differences are also minimal, because neither sex holds the values of aspiring politicians. As competition begins to increase, more traditional politicians begin to emerge among men, but competition still is not so keen as to prevent the candidacies of concerned female citizens. Because of these differing types, overall sex differences also begin to emerge. But at the more intense stages of competition recruitment strongly favors professionals, and consequently sex differences decline. There was only the slightest evidence of the "decline" stage in these data, but data on women legislators in other states provide some additional evidence for its existence.

It will be recalled that female and male legislators were examined only in New England because in other states there were too few women to make systematic comparisons; but one of the problems with the New England data was that very few of the women were professionals, and none were attorneys. My original hypothesis was that in more competitive situations women would not only have political careers comparable to men but would also tend to have "male" professional careers, and that the combined effect of the two would move such women in the direction of male behavior. Female lawyer-legislators are few in number, but all four of the women serving in New York were lawyers. Though these women differed among themselves, none reacted passively to the legislative environment. The questionnaire described in chapter 3 was also sent to all women legislators serving outside New England (see appendix 3 for further details), and among the 114 respondents 13, or 11.4 percent, were lawyers. Eleven, or 9.6 percent, listed their occupation as full-time legislator or politician. Clearly in states where women are less likely to be elected the few women who do succeed are more likely to follow typical male career patterns. There is also a suggestion that female lawyer-legislators, in comparison with nonlawyer females, may be somewhat more active in the legislature and somewhat less averse to legislative bargaining. Systematic comparisons are difficult because the absolute number of female lawyers is still very small, and the apparent differences are dependent on whether the lawyers are compared to all other female legislators or only to female legislators outside New England. Differences are quite sharp if the former comparison is made but are not so sharp if the latter comparison is made.* Female lawyer-legislators may differ behaviorally from nonlawyers (women who have followed the traditional law-to-politics route may be more prone to adopt "male" forms of behavior in the legislature), but the New England women also differ from their counterparts in the rest of the nation, as would be expected on the basis of the model developed here. Admittedly, one cannot conclude from these data that female legislators outside New England are more similar to male legislators; there is no direct evidence of the hypothesized third stage, and extreme caution is advised in making inferences on the basis of such measures used across a range of states differing in so many respects. But the data do suggest that in states where women are less likely to be elected, women

---

* Comparing lawyers to all other female legislators the gamma between "non-lawyer/lawyer" and activity is .36 and the gamma between "nonlawyer/lawyer" and bargaining is .45. Comparing lawyers only to female legislators outside New England the gamma for activity is .22 and for bargaining .16.

politicians, even those who are not lawyers, may be more prone to adopt "male" forms of behavior.[2]

Analysis of trends among the entire sample of women indicates one particularly interesting relationship worth noting here. All the women legislators were asked, "What are the special interests of women, if any?" Some indicated such issues as "health," "human services," and other traditional feminine issue areas; some indicated "equal pay for equal work"; and some indicated such things as "sex discrimination," "equality," "abortion," or "day care." The first two categories of women were no more prone to be favorably disposed toward legislative bargain-

Table 6.1 Bargaining, by Interest in Women's Rights

	Attitude toward Bargaining					
	1	2	3	4	Totals	N
Special Interest in Women's Rights						
No (%)	40	38	17	4	100	(104)
Yes (%)	20	39	32	8	100	(64)

Gamma = .39

Note: *1* indicates a negative attitude and *4* a positive attitude.

ing than those who did not mention such issues. However, women in the third category, legislators who mentioned what I will call women's rights issues, were considerably more favorably disposed toward bargaining than women who did not mention such issues (table 6.1). It would appear then that female legislators who are concerned with women's rights are more likely to adopt "male" forms of behavior.

Chapters 3 and 4 provided a more intensive exploration of sex roles in state legislatures. Four different areas were explored:

1. the general problems facing persons who simultaneously occupy the status of female and the status of state legislator;
2. the orientations individual women legislators develop;
3. the functions women serve; and

    4. the social and political consequences of allowing individuals to occupy both statuses.

With respect to the first area it was found that the female legislator's sex status is of consequence initially, and sometimes continually, in interactions with constituents, lobbyists, and colleagues. And as a result the female legislator acquires both disadvantages and opportunities. Most of the disadvantages derive from the unflattering images of women in the conventional culture, whereas most of the advantages or opportunities derive from the ideal images of women and the traditional courtesies associated with them. Some of the specific disadvantages are (1) difficulty in obtaining the nomination, (2) being perceived as ever available by constituents, (3) having to justify publicly how family responsibilities are handled, (4) being channeled into traditional feminine areas, and (5) being required to prove basic competence. Some of the specific advantages are (1) friendlier receptions in door-to-door campaigning, (2) greater maneuverability, for example, freedom to be more direct in seeking information, (3) lesser likelihood of being undercut by colleagues, (4) lesser liability to sanctions for breaking certain "rules of the game," and (5) being less subject to the arm-twisting of lobbyists.

    Typically the female legislator's family roles also have an impact on her legislative interactions. These roles often limit her political aspirations and in fact account for the common pattern of delaying entrance into political life until the most burdensome years of motherhood are over. It was also found, however, that her family roles may afford her a certain economic independence that permits her to be more independent politically. In addition, once a woman decides to take on the legislative role, she can often allocate more of her available time and resources to her legislative duties than a male legislator who is also a family breadwinner.

    With respect to the second area I found that four distinct patterns of adaptation to the legislative environment could be identified. A typology of four role types—"Housewife-Benchwarmer," "Traditional Civic Worker," "Women's Rights Advocate," and "Passive Women's Rights Advocate"—was derived from the interaction of two variables, self-image and attitude toward women's role in society. For each type the pattern of recruitment, commitment to politics, mode of legislative activity, and perception of sex-role salience are conditioned by the associated self-image and attitude. For example, the Housewife-Benchwarmer, who is typically plagued by self-doubt and is very comfortable with women's present role in society, is recruited for the legislature only where competition for legislative seats is practically nonexistent. Once in the legislature she does not become involved in the center of the legislative process, nor does she experience conflict between being a woman and a legislator.

With respect to the third area, I found that the functions served by women legislators are dependent on both the personal role conceptions of the individual women and the structural requirements of the legislature. The Housewife-Benchwarmer and Traditional Civic Worker both perform the traditional feminine emotional-expressive function and thus contribute to a lessening of interpersonal tensions in the legislature. The Traditional Civic Worker, because of her selfless public-service mode of activity, contributes to the instrumental needs of the legislature as well. In contrast, the Women's Rights Advocate, because of her career ambitions and interest in changing sex roles, may contribute to an increase in the tension level of the legislature. In addition, many women occupied chairmanship and vice-chairmanship positions in the New Hampshire house, not because they were exceptionally talented or aggressive, but because of the basic scarcity of talent. In Connecticut, the general level of talent being higher, no woman chaired any of the standing committees, and the two leadership positions that women held were obtained only after organized pressure by women on the male leadership.

Generalizations as to the social and political consequences of the presence of women in the legislature are highly tentative. The most apparent social consequence is that interactions be-

tween female and male legislators are mediated by the traditional courtesies that color interactions between the sexes outside the legislature. Women do not break into the "backslapping
camaraderie": there is considerable social segregation by sex.
Political consequences appear to be more dependent on the personal role conceptions of the women representatives than on the
actual number of women. If the women legislators are not interested in "acting for" women, then women's interests will not be
represented; the fact that there are women in the legislature
will be of no consequence for policy output. If, however, the
legislators hold orientations that motivate them to "act for"
women, the political consequences both internally—in terms of
organization—and externally—in terms of output and linkages
to activist groups—may be considerable. Sheer numbers are not
crucial. Substantive representation is not dependent on descriptive representation.

Do the findings that have been presented here allow me to
say anything with respect to the very general questions I posed
in the preface? Certain of the differences between the sexes in
terms of participation in politics have been documented. We
now know something beyond the basic difference that women
participate in politics less than men. The data also attest to the
powerful effect of historical precedent: where women participate today is very much a function of where they participated
yesterday. Ella Grasso, a former state legislator, was elected in
November 1974 to the governorship of the state of Connecticut.
She was the first woman governor ever elected who did not
succeed her husband. This event was heralded as a great
change in the ways of American politics; though I certainly do
not discount its significance and do not mean to suggest that
Governor Grasso does not possess unique qualities that account
for her success, the data here strongly suggest that this event
could not have taken place in any other state in the Union.

But the question of change—whether the differences are
changing—is what most intrigues me. Unfortunately, this is
where my data are weakest. There are some limited quantitative
data that indicate that differences are changing in the direction

of women becoming more like men. The interviews in part also suggest that this may be the case: the Women's Rights Advocate is certainly more similar to a traditional male politician than is the Housewife-Benchwarmer. The Women's Rights Advocate is ambitious and is likely to become somewhat more common. If a decline in sex differences simply means the wholesale adoption by women of male forms of behavior, the ultimate consequences would be, from both the human and feminist points of view (if these are not indeed identical), dubious to say the least. However, the Women's Rights Advocate is a complex role type. Her career pattern and educational background lead her to view men as her reference group, and in fact it is because of the "status disequilibrium" between her achieved status and her sex status that she becomes interested in changing women's role. But she is also acutely aware of the dangers of adopting *all* forms of male behavior, and she has not rejected all aspects of feminine culture. This awareness motivates her to modify the traditional professional legislator's role: for example, all of the Women's Rights Advocates who are lawyers suspended their private practices while in the legislature. The Women's Rights Advocate provides some hope that a decline in sex differences need not be one-way change. But as I indicated earlier, though her personal disposition might incline her one way, the structural demands of the legislature in combination with her assertive personality may lead another way.

There is, however, one other factor that needs to be considered in looking toward the future—the interaction between role types and organizational developments outside the legislature. Personal role conceptions develop in a social context: the structural demands of the legislature are part of this context, but the environment of the institution itself is another part. Activist groups outside can modify and influence the orientations of women serving in the legislature. An intriguing question is the role feminist organizations will play in helping the Women's Rights Advocate to resolve her conflict. If these organizations weaken, I see little chance that the Women's Rights Advocate will be able to resist the weight of institutional forces pulling

her in the direction of "male" patterns. But even if feminist organizations flourish and develop, it is important to consider the
direction of such development. One possible scenario is that of
strong, autonomous organizations providing support structures
that will enable female and male legislators to resist adoption of
the less desirable "male" characteristics and to retain desirable
"female" characteristics. New political procedures based on
shared public concerns rather than competition among narrow
special interests would be created, ultimately leading to the hu-
manization of the institution and society. Another possibility is
that activist feminist groups will lose their movement-like characteristics and evolve into traditional pressure groups arguing
for specific material benefits for their constituencies, relying on
all the conventional pressure techniques. If these groups were
"successful," the legislative process would roll on: the material
position of middle- and upper-class women would most likely
improve, but the domination of one group by another in society
at large would be intensified. Sex would no longer be a criterion
for domination, and so the criterion of class would hold full
sway.[3]

These scenarios provide starkly contrasting visions of the future.[4] In the midst of creating and evaluating real-world
strategies, it will prove difficult to assess accurately where particular choices will lead. Reforms by their very nature alter institutions and procedures within the prevailing system, and so the
charge may always be brought that such-and-such reform represents co-optation.[5] A purist approach, however, can lead to an
absence of program—the surest way to maintain the status quo.
I have been trying to demonstrate here that the consequences
of reforming legislative bodies so as to include more women are
not straightforward and are dependent on a variety of factors
(certainly, from a moral point of view, arguments for the equal
political participation of women should not be based on consequences); but integral to the question of how might women
behave is how many will there be? Is equality of numbers likely
to be realized in the near future? We saw in chapter 2 the
tremendous advances women have made in state legislatures

since the emergence of the contemporary women's movement. But we also saw that women are still very far from achieving political parity. When will this be achieved? If the proportion of women legislators continued to double during four-year intervals, parity would be achieved by 1984. (What was Orwell talking about?!) Is political equality really that close?

As the number of female candidacies increases—as women begin to develop more sophistication about campaign techniques and to find alternative sources of funding—the number of women in public office will surely increase. All these things are occurring as a consequence of the women's movement, but I think our exploration of the role choices faced by female legislators suggests that parity is a long way off.[6] Different legislators effect different modes of adaptation, and what is possible for one legislator is impossible for another because of differences in personality and values. But these orientations also evolve from legislative and social structures, and the frequency of the various types is conditioned by social conditions beyond the legislature. The family roles of women are rooted in a set of social conditions that force women with some interest in politics to make certain choices (we saw that these may often be unconscious), and these choices necessarily involve costs. The Traditional Civic Worker may forsake advanced political office, while the Women's Rights Advocate may forsake having children. Certain women may be able to work out individual solutions without seeming to incur costs because they have uniquely fortunate circumstances—wealth, a husband willing to forgo his career, and so forth—but the prevailing conditions are such that most women will not be so fortunate. My argument is that, given these conditions, the pool of women willing to incur the costs of political office will not provide enough candidates for the achievement of parity.[7] Numerical equality is much further along in New Hampshire than in New York, because in the former the lack of competition and the minimal demands of office make the costs negligible. The Advocate's orientation is one way of adapting to the rigors of office in New York, and the activity of feminist groups outside the legislature certainly contributes to the formation of this orientation. But costs are still involved, and so I think it unlikely that the pool of Advocates will become so large that Advocates will share the legislature with male legislators in the near future.

The only way then of making political office both feasible and attractive for large numbers of women (I certainly do not mean to imply here that all males have equal access to office; clearly differences of class among men are related to possibilities for office) is to restructure institutions in the larger society. Day-care facilities are often suggested as a policy alternative, but though their importance should not be minimized, the provision of day care, even if it were free, is not equivalent to equal sharing of child-care responsibilities. The phenomenon of "house-husbanding" may be, like women in politics, a popular topic for human interest stories, but it is anomalous. What is demanded is a fundamental change in work patterns, and this might involve rethinking the organization of most institutions. The ideology that supports a division between the domestic and public spheres would need to be rethought and the structural discontinuities between the two dissolved.[8] My contention is that such radical steps would interest majorities of men and women only if the domestic sphere were not devalued in the process of change.

I argued earlier that one should not necessarily expect that a legislature composed equally of men and women would operate very differently from one where men were dominant. I think the reader can now see that when women achieve equality in all political institutions the world will be a very different place.

Appendix 1: Profile of Women Legislators in the 1971–72 Session

Organizational Memberships:

34%	Democratic or Republican Women's Club
24%	Business and Professional Women's Club
22%	League of Women Voters
14%	American Association of University Women
12%	General Federation of Women's Clubs

(N = 190)

	Nation (%)	New England (%)	Non–New England (%)
Occupation			
Housewife	31	37	27
Professional	27	13	38
a. teachers	8	0	8
b. lawyers	7	0	7
	(N = 190)	(N = 76)	(N = 114)
Age			
21–39	12	7	15
40–49	25	19	29
50–59	31	38	27
60–69	26	22	29
70–over	6	14	1
	(N = 184)	(N = 72)	(N = 112)
Education			
High school or less	27	43	16
Some college	27	21	30
College degree	19	20	19
Some post-college	9	7	10
Advanced degree	19	9	25
	(N = 188)	(N = 76)	(N = 112)
Family Income ($)			
less than 9,999	16	34	6
10,000–14,999	11	11	12
15,000–19,999	14	19	12
20,000–24,999	19	13	22
25,000–over	39	23	49
	(N = 140)	(N = 53)	(N = 87)

Appendix 1: (*Continued*)

	Nation (%)	New England (%)	Non–New England (%)
Marital Status			
Married	66	60	71
Single	7	8	7
Widowed	19	24	16
Divorced	7	9	6
	(N = 190)	(N = 76)	(N = 114)
No. of Children			
0	13	9	15
1	14	14	13
2	30	28	31
3	23	23	22
4 or more	21	28	18
	(N = 178)	(N = 71)	(N = 107)

Note: New England refers only to Connecticut, Maine, New Hampshire, and Vermont.

Appendix 2: Women in State Legislatures

State	House				Senate	
	1971–72		1975–76		1971–72	1975–76
	No.	%	No.	%	No.	No.
Alabama	1	.9	1	.9	0	0
Alaska	3	7.5	7	17.5	1	2
Arizona	8	13.3	13	21.7	4	5
Arkansas	2	2.0	3	3.0	1	0
California	3	3.7	2	2.5	0	0
Colorado	5	7.7	13	20.0	1	3
Connecticut	18	10.2	22	14.6	2	4
Delaware	4	10.3	8	19.5	2	2
Florida	4	3.4	12	10.0	1	1
Georgia	2	1.0	8	4.4	0	1
Hawaii	3	5.8	6	11.7	1	4
Idaho	3	4.3	9	12.9	0	1
Illinois	3	1.7	12	6.8	1	3
Indiana	7	7.0	6	6.0	1	3
Iowa	6	6.0	10	10.0	2	4
Kansas	3	2.4	8	6.4	0	1
Kentucky	4	4.0	3	3.0	1	2
Louisiana	3	2.8	2	1.9	0	0
Maine	14	9.9	23	15.2	1	1
Maryland	8	5.6	16	11.3	4	3
Massachusetts	4	1.7	14	5.8	1	2
Michigan	7	6.4	9	8.2	0	0
Minnesota	1	.7	7	5.2	0	1
Mississippi	3	2.5	5	4.1	3	1
Missouri	8	4.9	11	6.7	0	1
Montana	1	1.0	10	10.0	1	4
Nebraska *					2	1
Nevada	5	12.5	4	10.0	1	3
New Hampshire	68	17.3	102	25.5	2	2
New Jersey	2	2.5	6	7.5	0	3
New Mexico	2	2.8	3	4.3	0	2
New York	3	2.0	6	4.0	0	3
North Carolina	2	1.7	13	10.8	0	2
North Dakota	4	4.1	13	12.7	0	3
Ohio	3	3.0	7	7.1	2	2

Appendix 2: (*Continued*)

State	House				Senate	
	1971–72		1975–76		1971–72	1975–76
	No.	%	No.	%	No.	No.
Oklahoma	3	3.0	5	4.9	0	1
Oregon	5	8.3	8	13.3	2	3
Pennsylvania	6	2.9	8	3.9	1	1
Rhode Island	3	3.0	7	7.0	0	2
South Carolina	2	1.6	7	5.6	0	0
South Dakota	3	4.0	7	10.0	0	4
Tennessee	2	2.0	4	4.0	0	1
Texas	1	.7	7	4.7	1	1
Utah	6	8.7	8	10.7	3	0
Vermont	18	12.0	21	14.0	0	1
Virginia	1	1.0	6	6.0	0	0
Washington	8	8.2	14	14.3	0	4
West Virginia	7	7.0	8	8.0	1	1
Wisconsin	3	3.0	9	9.1	1	1
Wyoming	2	3.3	6	9.7	0	1
Totals	289		519		45+	91+

* Nebraska's legislature is unicameral.

Appendix 3: Questionnaire

The questionnaire was pretested on a small sample of legislators during November 1971. In mid-December 1971 the questionnaire was mailed to all women state legislators and 186 male legislators in Connecticut, Maine, New Hampshire, and Vermont. The overall response rate was 58 percent. Nationwide the response rate among Democratic women was 48 percent, among Republican women 67 percent.

In New England, in order to insure an adequate number of responses from men, the questionnaire was sent to more men than women. As Table A.1 indicates, this caution proved unnecessary, for party, not sex, was the most important determinant of response rate. The party breakdown among male respondents was 28 percent Democratic and 72 percent Republican, while among the female respondents it was 26 percent Democratic and 74 percent Republican.

Table A.1 Response Rates for New England, by Sex

	Republicans		Democrats		
	Females	Males	Females	Males	Totals
Connecticut					
No. sent	11	15	8	12	
No. returned	9	10	6	8	33
Maine					
No. sent	8	12	7	12	
No. returned	7	9	3	5	24
New Hampshire					
No. sent	52	76	18	29	
No. returned	32	45	7	10	94
Vermont					
No. sent	13	18	8	12	
No. returned	8	14	4	8	34
Total					185
(Percentage returned)	(67)	(65)	(48)	(49)	(60)

Note: Return figures refer to usable returns.

Appendix 4: Construction of Scales

I. Bargaining Scale
   Three questionnaire items formed a unidimensional and cumulative scale (Guttman scale). The coefficient of reproducibility was .96 (a coefficient of higher than .9 is generally considered to indicate a valid scale).
   The items were ordered as follows:
   1. "Find it difficult to trade votes with other legislators" was the *most difficult* item. "Occasionally" was the cutting point. (Passed item if checked "occasionally" or "frequently"; failed item if checked "hardly ever" or "never".)
   2. "Legislative vote-swapping is morally objectionable and should be avoided in the legislature" was the *second most difficult* item. "Disagree somewhat" was the cutting point. (Passed item if checked "Disagree Somewhat" or "Disagree Strongly"; failed item is checked "Agree Strongly" or "Agree Somewhat.)
   3. "The public would be better served if there were no bargaining in the legislature" was the *least difficult* item. "Disagree Somewhat" was the cutting point.
   The "no opinion" category was treated as missing data.

II. Activity Scale
   Three questionnaire items formed a Guttman scale. The coefficient of reproducibility was .94.
   The items were ordered as follows:
   1. "Speak on floor" was the *most difficult* item. "Frequently" was the cutting point. (Passed item if checked "frequently"; failed item if "occasionally," "hardly ever," or "never" checked.)
   2. "Take an active part in major negotiations" was the *second most difficult* item. "Occasionally" was the cutting point. (Passed item if "occasionally" or "frequently" checked; failed if "hardly ever" or "never" checked.)
   3. "Question witnesses" was the *least difficult* item. "Occasionally" was the cutting point.

For an explanation of the general procedures used in constructing scales see: Norman H. Nie, Dale H. Bent, C. Hadlai Hull, *SPSS* (New York: McGraw Hill, 1970), pp. 196–204.

Appendix 5: Methodological Details of Interviews

The initial procedure for obtaining interview subjects was to select a group of potential interviewees from the legislators who had responded to the mailed questionnaire. Consideration was given to party background, activity in the legislature, and questions that tapped the legislators' perceptions of the salience of sex roles. After selection of a group of respondents that displayed considerable variation on these factors, letters were sent to ask for their cooperation in a personal interview, indicating that they would receive a call from me when I arrived in their state. Because the goal was to obtain a total of twenty to twenty-five interviews, in each state letters were sent to more legislators than I could hope to interview given my time limitations.

Fortuitous circumstances became part of the selection process when I arrived in each state. In a few cases I was unable to reach the potential interviewee on the phone; in a few cases appointments were cancelled; and in several cases subjects who had not been called were interviewed simply because they were available while I was in the legislative chambers. The basic operating procedure was to obtain the largest number of interviews in the time available, while attempting to obtain representation from each of the parties. I had some difficulty in obtaining interviews with Democrats in New Hampshire, as indicated in table A.2. In Connecticut, after being informed by one legislator of

Table A.2 Number of Women Interviewed

	Democratic		Republican	
	House	Senate	House	Senate
New Hampshire				
Total number of women serving	17	1	51	1
Number of interviewed	2	1	9	0
% interviewed	12	100	18	0
Connecticut				
Total number of women serving	8	0	9	2
Number interviewed	3	0	5	2
% interviewed	37		55	100

certain organizational efforts by the women in each of the parties, I made a special effort to interview the two women who had been appointed to house leadership positions as a result of these efforts.

The interviews in New Hampshire took place during the last week of February 1972, during a special session of the legislature. In Connecticut they took place in mid-March of 1972. The interviews were all conducted in the capitol buildings of each state during the legislative sessions and were generally held in unoccupied committee rooms, but in several cases (particularly in Connecticut) a quiet room was not available and the interview was subject to noise interference and interruptions. The average length was sixty minutes; one was abbreviated, lasting for only fifteen minutes, and several others lasted about ninety minutes. The interviews were tape-recorded, but in two cases the tape recorder was not operating properly and the interview was written up from memory. The subjects were all given the opportunity to indicate that they preferred that the interview not be recorded on a machine, but none displayed any hesitation about the procedure. There is no reason to believe that the use of a recording device introduced any special biases.

Appendix 6: Interview Schedule

I. Prelegislative experiences
1. When did you first get interested in politics?
   a. Were you active then?
   b. What were some of the things that interested you in it?
   c. Did your husband have any particular influence?
   d. Anyone else?
   e. (If children fully grown): Were you active when your children were growing up?
2. Could you describe the circumstances that led to your nomination for the legislature?
   a. With whom did you first discuss the nomination?
   b. When was it that you first talked with a party official about the nomination?
   c. How did that conversation go?
   d. How did you feel about the idea then?
3. In making up your mind about running, what factors did you take into account?
   a. What were some of the pros and cons, as you saw it then?
   b. (If family not mentioned): Were your family obligations a consideration?
   c. What was your husband's attitude?
   d. Which of these factors that you have mentioned had the most to do with your final decision?
4. Did you have any problems in securing the nomination?
   a. (If yes): Do you think any of these problems arose because you are a woman?
5. It's been said that women face special problems when campaigning for office; did you find this to be so?
   a. Are there any techniques that male candidates use that you felt were unavailable to you because you are a woman?
6. Did you enjoy any particular advantages because you are a woman?
7. Did your husband have any role in your campaign?
8. Did you feel that the party gave you the same support they would have given to a male candidate?

II. Initial legislative experiences
1. When you first entered the legislature, how did you feel about your committee assignments?
   a. Did you feel that you were directed toward committee assignments that are presumed to be interesting to women?
   b. Did you feel that you got less favorable committee assignments than freshman male legislators?
2. (If not in first term):
   a. How have you felt about your committee assignments since your first term?
   b. Have you ever felt that you were not considered for certain committee posts or leadership positions because you are a woman?
      1. (If yes): What was the situation?
                   How did you feel about it?
                   What did you do?
      2. (If no): Do you know of any female acquaintances who have felt discriminated against in this way?

III. Role definitions
1. How would you describe the job of being a legislator—that is, what are the most important things you should be doing here?
   a. What is your main duty or function here?
   b. (Women's interests not mentioned): Are you particularly concerned about representing the interests of women?
      1. (If yes): What have you done in this area?
      2. (If no): Have you ever felt pressured to do so?
2. Thinking of these various points, how do you think you have done so far as a legislator?
   a. Which of these things do you think you have been more successful in doing?
   b. Which of them have given you trouble?
   c. What would you say has helped you personally in doing these things?
   d. What have been some of the things that have hindered you?
   e. Has being a woman ever hindered you? (If yes): Could you describe such a situation?
   f. Has being a woman ever helped you? (If yes): Could you describe such a situation?
3. Are there any particular tactics or strategies you can employ in achieving your legislative aims which are not available to male legislators?
4. Are there any tactics or strategies that male legislators employ that you feel are not available to you because you are a woman?
People have said that women in politics are under unique pressures. I would like to go into these with you.

5. Have you ever felt any special pressures or demands on you because you are a woman?
   1. (If yes): a. Does this occur often?
                b. What kinds of demands or pressures are they?
                c. How do you feel in this situation?
                d. What did you do?
                e. What were the consequences?
(Explore, if possible, each of above questions with respect to: party leaders; other legislators; constituents; lobbyists.)
6. It has been said that being a woman and being a legislator can come into conflict. Have you ever found yourself in such a situation?
   1. (if yes): a. Does this kind of situation occur often?
                b. Could you tell me about some of these situations?
                c. What kinds of difficulties did you experience?
                d. What did you do?
                e. What were the consequences?
   2. (If no): a. Do you know of any acquaintances who have been in this kind of situation?
                b. Are there any particular reasons why you have been able to avoid these situations?
(Explore questions with respect to all possible relationships.)
7. It's been said that every legislature has its unofficial rules of the game—certain things members must do and things they must not do if they want the respect and cooperation of fellow members? Are there any such rules which apply to the proper role of women in the legislature?
   a. How do you feel about them?
   b. What occurs when they are not followed?
IV. Legislative behavior
Now I would like you to elaborate on some of your responses to the questionnaire.
   1. In the questionnaire you said that you———speak on the floor. How do you feel when you speak there?
   2. How do you feel when you speak in committees?
   3. In the questionnaire you said that you———influence committee deliberations. Why do you think this is so?
      a. Have you ever tried to influence the deliberations and felt you were unsuccessful?
      b. (If frequently checked on questionnaire): Why do you think you have been so successful in influencing committee deliberations?
   4. By the way, what is your general reaction to committee work?

      a. Is there anything particular that stands out in your mind about it?

5. In the questionnaire you said that you are not usually excluded from the informal gatherings of male legislators. Are you usually invited or are you usually just not interested in attending?

      a. (If excluded and hindered checked): How do you feel your exclusion has hindered your effectiveness as a legislator?

      b. (If excluded and no effect): Why do you feel that this exclusion has had no bearing on your effectiveness as a legislator?

6. With whom do you most frequently discuss legislative matters?

7. Do you get together with other legislators outside of the regular sessions and committee meetings?

      a. Do you see other members outside of the capitol?

8. Since you've been in the legislature, have you ever been advised to act more feminine?

      1. (If yes): By whom?

                What was the situation?

                How did you feel?

9. Have you ever had any hesitancy about revealing your intellectual equality or superiority to men?

      1. (If yes):   Could you describe the siatuation?

      2. (If no):   Have other woman legislators ever expressed such hesitancy to you?

10. People have said that women who attain leadership positions often defer to their male colleagues. Have you found this to be so in the legislature?

V. Ideological orientations

Next I would like to ask you some questions about your thinking on women and the world of politics.

1. What would you say are the major problems women have had to face in politics?

2. Do you think that there are any strategies that might be pursued to lessen these problems?

3. Have you ever felt unable to accept certain responsibilities because of familial obligations?

4. What kind of advice would you give another woman who was just starting out in politics?

      a. What qualifications do you think a woman candidate should have?

5. Are you particularly interested in seeing more women run for political office?

1. (If yes): Why?
   a. What kinds of things do you think should be done to bring this about?
   b. Have you personally done anything?
   c. What will the consequences be if there is greater participation of women in political life?
2. (If no): Could you explain your reasoning?
6. How do you feel about the women's movement today?
   a. What do you see as its goals?
   b. What do you like about it?
   c. What don't you like about it?
      (If positive attitude has been expressed):
      1. What can the women's movement accomplish through political action?
      2. Some people say the movement should not concentrate exclusively on the issue of equal pay for equal work, but should devote more time to women's role in society—concentrating on techniques to alter women's self-image. How do you feel about these issues?

VI. Future perspectives
   1. What is your general feeling about politics in your own future?
      a. What would you say are some of the more likely political possibilities for you in the future?
      b. What are some of the less likely possibilities?
   2. Now in making your decisions about these possibilities, what are some of the factors you will be taking into account?
   3. How do these pros and cons add up to you now?

Appendix 7: Multivariate Analysis of State Differences in Percentage of Female Legislators

Dependent Variable	Independent Variables	Regression Coefficient	Standard Error	t Value
1. % female house 1971	seats per 100,000 1950–70 (logged)	.018	.005	3.29
	% female house 1961	.42	.10	4.14
	C	−.001		
	$r^2 = .49$			
2. % female house 1971	seats per 100,000 1950–70 (logged)	.017	.005	3.18
	% female house 1961	.37	.10	3.61
	South	−.02	.009	−2.12
	C	.008		
	$r^2 = .54$			
3. % female house 1975	seats per 100,000 1950–70 (logged)	.026	.008	3.23
	% female house 1961	.51	.15	3.37
	South	−.02	.015	−1.56
	C	.028		
	$r^2 = .50$			
4. % female house 1975	seats per 100,000 1950–70 (logged)	.027	.008	3.35
	% female house 1961	.57	.15	3.84
	C	.018		
	$r^2 = .48$			

Notes

Chapter 1

1. Margaret Mead, *Sex and Temperament in Three Primitive Societies*, 1963 ed. (New York: William Morrow), p. 302.
2. Angus Campbell et al., *The American Voter* (New York: John Wiley, 1964), pp. 256–58; Maurice Duverger, *The Political Role of Women* (Paris: UNESCO, 1955), p. 215; Harriet Holter, *Sex Roles and Social Structure* (Oslo: Universitetsforlaget, 1970), pp. 101, 102; Elina Haavio-Mannila, "Sex Roles in Politics," *Scandinavian Political Studies* 5 (1970), pp. 213–16; Ingunn Norderval Means, "Women in Local Politics: The Norwegian Experience," *Canadian Journal of Political Science* 5 (September 1972), pp. 365–88.
3. Haavio-Mannila, "Sex Roles in Politics," pp. 229–31; Ingunn Norderval Means, "Political Recruitment of Women in Norway," *Western Political Quarterly* 25 (September 1972), p. 492; Means, "Women in Local Politics," pp. 368–70.
4. Of the 41 women who were elected on their own through the Ninety-second Congress, 27 came from highly urbanized states:

New York, 8;	Michigan, 2;
Illinois, 5;	Indiana, 2;
California, 2;	Massachusetts, 2;
New Jersey, 2;	Pennsylvania, 1.

5. "The distribution of female and male workers by major occupation reveals striking differences between the two groups. In 1971, over 60 percent of female white-collar workers (more than one-third of all employed women) worked in clerical jobs. Yet almost 70 percent of male white-collar workers (28 percent of the male work force) were in either the professional and technical or the managerial category. . . . Men also have the highest-status, highest paying blue-collar jobs. Only 8 percent of women blue-collar workers (1.3 percent of the employed women) were craftsmen or foremen in 1971. Yet over 43 percent of the men in this group (20 percent of the male labor force) were categorized as craftsmen and foremen. . . . Women are heavily concentrated in an extremely small number of occupations . . . half of all working women were em-

ployed in just twenty-one of the 250 occupations listed by the Bureau of the Census in 1969. . . . The pay differentials between men and women parallel the occupational differences. Statistics for full-time, year-round employees show that in 1971 the median annual income was $9399 for men and $5593 for women. . . . Occupations in which women predominate are often dismissed as unskilled or unimportant, even for men." Report of the Twentieth Century Fund Task Force on Women and Employment, *Exploitation from 9 to 5* (New York: Twentieth Century Fund, 1975), pp. 48–53.

6. Charles S. Hyneman, "Tenure and Turnover of Legislative Personnel," *Annals of the American Academy of Political and Social Science* 195 (1935), pp. 21–31; Frank J. Sorauf, *Party and Representation* (New York: Atherton Press, 1963).

7. I am excluding here the situations of the multifactional South, where the legislature is nonprofessional, but competition may be very great because entry to the legislature is often a way to a fast buck.

8. Charles G. Bell and Charles M. Price, "Pre-Legislative Sources of Representational Roles," *Midwest Journal of Political Science* 12 (May 1960), pp. 254–70.

9. Hope Chamberlin, *A Minority of Members Women in the U.S. Congress* (New York: Praeger, 1973), pp. 352–55.

10. Charles S. Bullock, III, and Patricia Lee Findley Heys, "Recruitment of Women for Congress: A Research Note," *Western Political Quarterly,* September 1972, p. 420.

Chapter 2

1. Austin Ranney, "Parties in State Politics," in *Politics in the American States,* ed. Herbert Jacob and Kenneth N. Vines (Boston: Little Brown, 1965), pp. 63–64; V. O. Key, Jr., *American State Politics: An Introduction* (New York: Alfred A. Knopf, 1956), pp. 97–104; Joseph A. Schlesinger, "A Two-Dimensional Scheme for Classifying the States According to Degree of Inter-Party Competition," *American Political Science Review* 44 (1955), pp. 1120–28; Belle Zeller, ed., *American State Legislatures* (New York: Thomas Y. Crowell, 1954), pp. 199–211; Richard E. Dawson and James A. Robinson, "Inter-Party Competition, Economic Variables, and Welfare Policies in the American States," *Journal of Politics* 25 (1963), pp. 265–89.

2. Morrigene Van Helden, *Women in the U.S. Congress,* Congressional Research Service, Library of Congress, April 21, 1971, p. i.

3. Here I am interpreting the regression coefficient for the bivariate

equation of proportion of women in senates (Y) and proportion of women in lower houses (X). Y = − .005 + .608 X. r² = .49.

4. The explained variance for the equation which uses the logged value of seats per 100,000 persons is reported here because the logarithmic transformation makes the relationship less sensitive to the outlying values of New Hampshire and Vermont. Y = .009 + .023 log X. Logging a variable pulls the few extremely large values in toward the mean and spreads out the many smaller values which are clustered at the other end of the scale.

5. Duane Lockard, *New England State Politics* (Chicago: Henry Regenry, Gateway Edition, 1968), p. 5.

6. Robert A. Dahl and Edward R. Tufte, *Size and Democracy* (Stanford: Stanford University Press, 1973), p. 81.

7. For the simple bivariate regression between salary and percentage women the r² equals 11 percent. However when salary is entered with seats per 100,000 persons in the same regression the explained variance does not increase appreciably and the t value of salary drops sharply, indicating that salary is no longer significant. The healthy correlation between salary and seats per 100,000 persons (r = − .60) suggests a damaging degree of multicollinearity. (Multicollinearity is the statistical term used to describe the situation in which two or more explanatory variables are intercorrelated, making it impossible to assess their independent impacts on the dependent variable.)

8. J. W. Tukey and M. B. Wilk, "Data Analysis and Statistics: Techniques and Approaches," in *The Quantitative Analysis of Social Problems*, ed. Edward R. Tufte (Reading, Mass.: Addison-Wesley, 1970), p. 371.

9. Ann Scott, *The Southern Lady: From Pedestal to Politics, 1830–1930* (Chicago: University of Chicago Press, 1970).

10. Hope Chamberlin, *A Minority of Members: Women in the U.S. Congress* (New York: Praeger, 1973).

11. For the period 1955–60 there were 1,157,937 "immigrants" (persons moving into the state from other states) into the state. In 1960 60 percent of Florida's population was born in another state. U.S., Bureau of the Census, U.S. Census of Population 1960, Subject Reports State of Birth PC (2)-2A, Tables 11 and 25.

12. Florida elected a Republican governor in 1966 and a Republican U.S. senator in 1968 and has voted Republican in all presidential elections since 1952 except for the 1964 election. Richard M. Scammon, ed., *America at the Polls: The Vote for President, 1920–64* (Pittsburgh: Governmental Affairs Institute, University of Pittsburgh Press, 1965), p. 48.

13. In 1960 the percentage of foreign-born in Rhode Island was 10.0

percent, in Connecticut 10.9 percent, and in Massachusetts 11.2 percent; the percentage of natives of mixed parentage was 29.5 percent in Rhode Island, 27.5 percent in Connecticut, and 28.8 percent in Massachusetts. U.S., Bureau of the Census, U.S. Census of Population 1960, Subject Reports Nativity and Parentage PC (2)-1A, Table 15.

14. Lockard, *New England State Politics*, p. 228.
15. For example, in 1965 there were a total of 44 representatives from Litchfield County (population 119,856), and 7 were women (6 Republicans, 1 Democrat). In 1967 Litchfield County's total number of representatives was down to 9, and 1 was a woman.
16. Lockard, *New England State Politics*, p. 152.
17. Ibid., pp. 178, 179. The Rhode Island house of representatives ranked thirty-third on the Schubert-Press index of malapportionment (David Brady and Douglas Edmonds, *The Effects of Malapportionment on Policy Output in the American States* [Iowa City: Laboratory for Political Research, University of Iowa, 1966]).
18. Percentage of urban dwellers in 1960:

Rhode Island	86.4
Massachusetts	83.6
Connecticut	78.3
New Hampshire	58.3
Maine	50.8
Vermont	38.5

U.S., Bureau of the Census, U.S. Census of Population 1970, Number of Inhabitants PC (1)-1A U.S. Summary, Table 18. Lockard, *New England State Politics*, pp. 172, 173.

19. Lockard, *New England State Politics*, p. 190; Herbert Gans, *The Urban Villagers* (New York: Free Press of Glencoe, 1962); Melvin Kohn, *Class and Conformity: A Study in Values* (Homewood, Ill.: Dorsey Press, 1969), pp. 91–126; Susan Orden, "Working Wives and Marriage Happiness," *American Journal of Sociology* 74 (January 1969); Lee Rainwater, Richard Coleman, and Gerald Handel *Workingman's Wife* (New York: Oceana Publications, 1959).
20. Arizona ranked thirty-sixth on both the David-Eisenberg and Schubert-Press indexes of malapportionment (Brady and Edmonds, *Malapportionment*).
21. Jacob and Vines, *Politics in the American States*, p. 165.
22. From 1923 to 1951, 38 terms were served by Democratic women and 4 terms were served by Republican women. The average number of women serving per term was 2.9. Terms, rather than actual numbers of women who served, are given because data prior to 1953 do not allow for computation of individuals. Number-per-term rather than percentages are also used because of limitations on data in this period.

23. Daniel Elazar, *American Federalism*, 2nd ed. (New York: Thomas Y. Crowell, 1972), pp. 85, 90, 93–104, 136.
24. Ibid., pp. 96–98 (emphasis added).
25. Of the persons who moved into Arizona between 1955 and 1960 13 percent were age 55 and above; during the period 1965–70 17 percent were age 55 and above. U.S., Bureau of the Census, Census of Population 1960, Mobility for States and Economic Areas; Census of Population 1970, Mobility for States and the Nation.
26. Elazar, *American Federalism*, Table 18, p. 136, p. 113.
27. Ibid., pp. 99, 94, 95.
28. Yet because Elazar's idea of the moralistic subculture is so intriguing I did attempt a crude operationalization of the concept by creating a dummy variable for moralism. Each state was assigned a score of "1" if it had a moralistic strain in its prevailing culture and a score of "0" if it did not have such a strain. This operationalization of moralism explained 15 percent of the variation (Pearson R correlation of .39). Moralism (according to Elazar) is characteristic of states that emphasize mass participation. It is correlated with both the competition measure and the proportion of women in 1960, and hence in the multivariate model its coefficient was not significant. Ira Sharkansky (in "The Utility of Elazar's Political Culture," *Polity* 2 [Fall 1969], pp. 66–83) assigns numerical values to the different combinations in Elazar's designations of prevailing cultures. Sharkansky derives an interval scale going from the moralist to the individualist to the traditionalist. If this measure is used here it explains 11 percent of the variation in the proportion of women.
29. Inclusion of the South in analyses based on all the states is often a source of controversy in the state politics literature (see Jack L. Walker and Dennis D. Riley's communication to the editor, *American Political Science Review* 63 (1969), pp. 900–03). Interestingly, if a parameter for Democratic domination of the legislature is included in the equation it is significant (the more Democratic, the lower the percentage of women). However, if the southern states are excluded Democratic partisanship drops out. Fortunately the coefficients for the seats ratio and the percentage of women in 1960 remain significant even when the southern states are excluded from the equation.
30. All states except Kentucky, Louisiana, Mississippi, New Jersey, and Virginia hold their legislative elections in even years, so the 1974 elections are the most recent for the nation as a whole. The 1974 campaign was also the first in which the National Women's Political Caucus conducted a full-scale effort to elect more women to public office.
31. I am emphasizing absolute numbers because the relatively small

size of senates may make proportions somewhat misleading here.

32. The coefficient for the South is not significant in 1975. See appendix 7.

33. I did attempt some exploration of the consequences of state women's political caucus activities, but this proved to be an impossible task with the data I had available (questionnaire responses from a survey of state caucuses and conversations with caucus activists). In North Carolina a state caucus was formed about the same time as the National Women's Political Caucus (July 1971), and considerable organizational development has taken place during the ensuing years—there being 6 active and functioning local caucuses prior to the 1974 election. Several caucus members successfully ran for the legislature, and others worked in the campaigns. A strong case can be made that the increase from 2 women in the 1971 session to 15 in the 1975 session is attributable to caucus activities. And yet in California, where the caucus also dates back to 1971 and is very active, the number of female legislators declined from 3 in 1971 to 2 in 1975. Only better data and the passage of time will allow for systematic generalizations.

34. There is every reason to believe that the increases in all the states took place because more women ran for office and not because of a sudden increase in the election rates of women legislative candidates. Unfortunately there are no data available for the 1970 election, but the National Women's Political Caucus estimates that there were 917 women candidates for state houses and state senates in 1972 and 1,207 in 1974. The election rate in 1974 for women candidates was 64 percent in New Hampshire, 55 percent in Colorado, and 52 percent in Montana. The nationwide rate, excluding these 3 states, was 45 percent.

35. *Dictionary of American Biography,* Supplement VI, forthcoming; S.V. "Blair, Emily Newell"; Emily Newell Blair, "Why I am Discouraged About Women in Politics," *Women's Journal* 16 (January 1931). I am indebted to Estelle B. Freedman for directing me to Mrs. Blair.

Chapter 3

1. James David Barber, *The Lawmakers* (New Haven: Yale University Press, 1965), pp. 26–27.

2. In Emmy E. Werner and Louise Bachtold, "Personality Characteristics of Women in American Politics" (Paper presented at the 1972 Annual Meeting of the American Political Science Association, Washington, D.C., September 1972), comparisons are made between women legislators who served in the 1970–71 state legis-

latures and "elected male leaders" from a study published in 1954; in Edmond Constantini and Kenneth H. Craik, "Women as Politicians: The Social Background, Personality, and Political Careers of Female Party Leaders" (*Journal of Social Issues*, vol. 28, no. 2 [1972], p. 219), sex comparisons are made among congressmen, state legislators, delegates to national conventions, and county chairmen.

3. M. Kent Jennings and Norman Thomas, "Men and Women in Party Elites: Social Roles and Political Resources," *Midwest Journal of Political Science* 12 (November 1968).

4. Kenneth Prewitt, *The Recruitment of Political Leaders: A Study of Citizen-Politicians*, (Indianapolis: Bobbs-Merrill, 1970), p. 96.

5. Fred Greenstein, *Children and Politics*, rev. ed. (New Haven: Yale University Press, 1969), chap. 6; Robert D. Hess and Judity V. Torney, *The Development of Political Attitudes in Children* (Garden City, N.Y.: Doubleday, Anchor Books, 1968), chap. 8. These differences may, however, be disappearing among children today. See Anthony M. Orum, Roberta S. Cohen, Sherri Grasmuck, and Amy Orum, "Sex Socialization and Politics," *American Sociological Review* 39 (April 1974), pp. 197–209.

6. Walter Mischel, "Sex-Typing and Socialization," in *Carmichael's Manual of Child Psychology*, ed. Paul H. Mussen, 3rd ed. (New York: John Wiley, 1970).

7. Prewitt, *Recruitment of Political Leaders*, p. 66; Dwaine Marvick and Charles R. Nixon, "Recruitment Contrasts in Rival Campaign Groups," in Dwaine Marvick, ed., *Political Decision Makers* (New York: Free Press of Glencoe, 1961); Richard E. Dawson and Kenneth Prewitt, *Political Socialization* (Boston: Little Brown, 1969); Heinz Eulau and John D. Sprague, *Lawyers in Politics* (New York: Bobbs-Merrill, 1964).

8. Donald Matthews, *The Social Background of Political Decision-Makers* (Garden City: Doubleday, 1954); Prewitt, *Recruitment of Political Leaders*, p. 89; Barber, *The Lawmakers*.

9. U.S., Department of Labor, Women's Bureau, *Why Women Work* (Washington, D.C.: U.S. Government Printing Office, 1972).

10. Marjorie Lansing, "Sex Differences in Voting and Activism" (Paper presented at the Annual Meeting of the American Political Science Association, Chicago, September 1971); Robert Lane, *Political Life* (New York: Free Press, Paperback ed., 1965), chap. 15.

11. Jennings and Thomas, "Men and Women in Party Elites," p. 479.

12. Ibid., p. 476.

13. "Legislators are concentrated in prestigious occupations. A great majority of legislators are either engaged in the professions, or are proprietors, managers, or officials of business. . . . lawyers are the

largest single occupational group." Thomas R. Dye, "State Legislative Politics," in *Politics in the American States,* ed. Herbert Jacob and Kenneth N. Vines, 2nd ed. (Boston: Little Brown, 1971), pp. 178–79.

14. Jennings and Thomas ("Men and Women in Party Elites," p. 477) also find no difference in the educational achievement levels of employed and nonemployed females.

15. Obviously these income differences are also a result of the fact that none of these females are lawyers and, of those who are employed, very few hold professional jobs.

16. Jennings and Thomas, "Men and Women in Party Elites," p. 477; Constantini and Craik, "Women as Politicians," p. 220.

17. Jennings and Thomas, "Men and Women in Party Elites," p. 479.

18. Prewitt, *Recruitment of Political Leaders,* p. 59.

19. In the Jennings and Thomas study women were also slightly more active than men in contacting voters and distributing literature, but men were considerably more active in making speeches and in campaign management. The first two activities are clearly women's activities, whereas it would appear that sex differences with respect to the latter two activities may vary with the nature of campaigns.

20. Jennings and Thomas, "Men and Women in Party Elites," p. 481.

21. Barber (*The Lawmakers,* pp. 238–39) discusses how change and growth in a district introduce uncertainties into the recruiter's calculations. "The next election might be an upset. Concurrently, the supply of potential candidates expands. . . . Mere willingness to take a candidacy declines as an important criterion, while the salable characteristics of potential candidates gains significance."

22. Of the 20 Democratic women 2 came from "safe Democrat" and 5 from "mostly Democrat" districts, and of the 31 Democratic men 12 came from "safe Democrat" and 10 from "mostly Democrat" districts.

23. Jennings and Thomas, "Men and Women in Party Elites," p. 487 (emphasis added).

24. The legislators were asked to place themselves on a scale concerning how they made decisions; the respective poles were: "Rely on advice of others with more experience or ability," which had the value "1," and "Figure most things out for myself to the best of my ability," which had the value "7." Eighteen percent of the males placed themselves at "7," while this was true of 8 percent of the women. Gamma = − .16.

25. Kenneth Prewitt ("Political Ambitions, Volunteerism, and Electoral Accountability," *American Political Science Review* 64 [March 1970], p. 14) observes that "where the methods of selecting and

displacing political leaders encourage the norm of volunteerism, electoral accountability is weakened. Volunteers with no political ambitions feel quite free to vote their conscience and vote against the majority." Prewitt obviously feels that this situation is undesirable.

26. These indirect indicators were chosen rather than the item which asked the respondents to classify the competitiveness of their districts with respect to state legislative contests because, as we have seen, this item is more a measure of party difference with respect to nominations than of seat competition.

27. Eighty percent of the women and 78 percent of the men who sought their seats had been involved in party politics before becoming legislators, while this was true of 72 percent of the women and 60 percent of the men who were asked to run; 55 percent of the women and 52 percent of the men who sought their seats had held some party office, while this was true of only 36 percent of the women and 31 percent of the men who were asked to run.

28. Jennings and Thomas, "Men and Women in Party Elites," p. 483.

29. According to Schlesinger's theory of political ambition, current behavior is a response to future office goals. See Joseph A. Schlesinger, *Ambition and Politics* (Chicago: Rand McNally, 1966), p. 6.

30. Twenty percent of the Republican women have annual *family* incomes of $25,000 and over, while this is true of only 5 percent of the Democrats.

31. It should be noted here that one way these states vary is in the proportion of retired persons. I have repeatedly stressed the association between retired persons and women, but in fact this is the case in only 3 of the states. In the Connecticut sample there was only one retired person. This association was true in Connecticut prior to reapportionment but is not today. Women appear to have weathered the changes wrought by reapportionment better than retired persons.

Chapter 4

1. Daniel J. Levinson, "Role, Personality and Social Structure in the Organizational Setting," in *Contemporary Analytical Theory*, ed. David E. Apter and Charles F. Andrain (Englewood Cliffs, N.J.: Prentice-Hall, 1972), p. 563; Jean Lipman-Bluman, "Role De-Differentiation as a System Response to Crisis: Occupational and Political Roles of Women" (Menlo Park, Cal.: Stanford Research Institute, 1973), p. 4; Neal Gross, Ward S. Mason, and Alexander McEachern, *Explorations in Role Analysis: Studies of the School*

200 *Notes*

Superintendency Role (New York: John Wiley, 1958), p. 4; Shirley S. Angrist, "The Study of Sex Roles," *Journal of Social Issues* 25 (January 1969), p. 216.

2. George Herbert Mead, *Mind, Self and Society* (Chicago: University of Chicago Press, 1934); Ralph Linton, *The Study of Man* (New York: D. Appleton-Century, 1936).
3. Talcott Parsons, *The Social System* (Glencoe: Free Press, 1951); Robert H. Merton, *Social Theory and Social Structure* (Glencoe: Free Press, 1957).
4. John C. Wahlke et al., *The Legislative System* (New York: John Wiley, 1962), p. 8.
5. Levinson ("Role, Personality and Social Structure," p. 572) points out the necessity for taking personality needs into account.
6. James David Barber, *The Lawmakers* (New Haven: Yale University Press, 1965).
7. Levinson, "Role, Personality and Social Structure," p. 566.
8. Ibid., p. 567.
9. Gross, Mason, and McEachern, *Explorations in Role Analysis*, p. 48, discusses the difference in connotation between position and status.
10. Marcia Millman, "Observations on Sex Role Research," *Journal of Marriage and the Family* 33 (November 1971), p. 773.
11. Michael Banton, *Roles: An Introduction to the Study of Social Relations* (New York: Basic Books, 1965), pp. 30, 34 (second and third quotations).
12. Simone de Beauvoir, *The Second Sex* (New York: Alfred A. Knopf, Bantam Books, 1952), p. xv.
13. Gross, Mason, and McEachern, *Explorations in Role Analysis*, p. 244; Theodore M. Newcomb, Ralph H. Turner, and Philip E. Converse, *Social Psychology: The Study of Human Interaction* (New York: Holt, Rinehart, and Winston, 1965), p. 404.
14. William J. Goode, "A Theory of Role Strain," *American Sociological Review* 25 (August 1960), p. 485.
15. William C. Mitchell, "Occupational Role Strains: The American Elective Public Official," *Administrative Science Quarterly*, September 1958, p. 220.
16. Ibid., pp. 221, 219 (second and third quotations).
17. Ibid., p. 221.
18. Cynthia Fuchs Epstein, *Woman's Place: Options and Limits in Professional Careers* (Berkeley and Los Angeles: University of California Press, 1971), pp. 20, 22–23.
19. The 1972 Harris Poll indicates that the public is much more favorably disposed to the idea of women as judges than to the idea of

women in electoral positions. Louis Harris and Associates, *The 1972 Virginia Slims American Women's Opinion Poll* (New York: Louis Harris and Associates, n.d.), p. 46.

20. Wahlke et al. (*The Legislative System*, p. 147) list "Negotiation: Recognize the necessity and/or acceptability of log-rolling, horse-trading, swapping-out" as one of the "rules of the game" perceived by legislators.

21. Barbara Welter, "The Cult of True Womanhood," in Wendy Martin, ed., *The American Sisterhood* (New York: Harper and Row, 1972), p. 245.

22. Lotte Bailyn, "Notes on the Role of Choice in the Psychology of Professional Women," in Robert Jay Lifton, ed., *The Woman in America* (Boston: Beacon Press, 1967), pp. 242, 243.

23. Though I emphasize the difference between private and public solutions, this difference should not be confused with that between individual and collective solutions. Both solutions here are individual solutions, and in fact it is the very lack of collective or societal solutions that places special burdens on such women.

24. Harriet Holter, *Sex Roles and Social Structure*, (Oslo: Universitetsforlaget, 1970), p. 113.

25. Gross, Mason, and McEachern (*Explorations in Role Analysis*, pp. 244–46) discuss the situation of role incumbents who are unaware of incompatible expectations.

26. Banton, *Roles*, p. 33.

27. Holter, *Sex Roles*, pp. 167, 168.

28. Sandra L. Bem and Daryl J. Bem, "Training the Woman to Know Her Place: The Power of a Non-conscious Ideology," in Michele Garskof, ed., *Roles Women Play: Readings Toward Women's Liberation* (Belmont, Cal.: Brooks/Cole, 1971), pp. 92–93.

29. Holter, *Sex Roles*, p. 38.

30. Peggy Lamson, *Few Are Chosen* (Boston: Houghton Mifflin Co., 1968), p. xxiii. See also Susan Tolchin and Martin Tolchin, *Clout: Womanpower and Politics* (New York: Coward, McCann & Geoghegan, 1973), p. 62.

31. Lamson, *Few Are Chosen*, p. xxiii.

32. Goode, "Theory of Role Strain," p. 486.

33. Epstein, *Woman's Place*, pp. 99, 100.

34. Harris (*Virginia Slims Opinion Poll*, p. 36) reports that 17 percent of women and 7 percent of men would be *more likely* to vote for women candidates for president if the women were running against equally qualified men.

35. It will be recalled from chapter 2 that the biennial legislative salary in New Hampshire is $200. In Connecticut at the time these in-

terviews were conducted the annual salary was $2,000 with a $1,500 biennial expense allowance during the session and a $1,500 biennial expense allowance between sessions (legislative salaries have since been raised in Connecticut).

36. Kenneth Prewitt (*The Recruitment of Political Leaders: A Study of Citizen-Politicians* [Indianapolis: Bobbs-Merrill, 1970], p. 31) summarizes an unpublished paper of Verba's.

37. Epstein, *Woman's Place*, pp. 191 (emphasis added), 192.

38. See Graham Staines, Carol Tarvis, and Toby Epstein Jayaratne, "The Queen Bee Syndrome," *The Female Experience*, special issue of *Psychology Today* (1973).

39. Helen Mayer Hacker, "Women as a Minority Group," *Social Forces* 30 (October 1951), p. 61.

40. Epstein, *Woman's Place*, p. 26.

41. Johan Galtung, "A Structural Theory of Aggression," in Ivo K. Feierabend, Rosalind L. Feierabend, and Ted Robert Gurr, eds., *Anger, Violence, and Politics* (Englewood Cliffs, N.J.: Prentice-Hall, 1972), pp. 86–88.

42. Joseph A. Schlesinger, *Ambition and Politics* (Chicago: Rand McNally, 1966), p. 6.

43. Barber, *The Lawmakers*, p. 69.

44. Wahlke et al., *The Legislative System*, p. 325.

45. L. Harman Zeigler and Michael A. Baer, "The Recruitment of Lobbyists and Legislators," *Midwest Journal of Political Science* 12 (1968), p. 493.

46. This "males-only policy was permanently relaxed after March 16, 1973, one of the first casualties resulting from the Assembly's ratification of the Equal Rights Amendment." Tolchin and Tolchin, *Clout: Womanpower and Politics*, p. 106.

47. Carol Lopate, *Women in Medicine* (Baltimore: Johns Hopkins Press, 1968); Margaret M. Poloma, "Role Conflict and the Married Professional Woman," in Constantina Safilios-Rothschild, ed., *Toward a Sociology of Women* (Lexington, Mass.: Xerox Corp., 1972).

48. Epstein, *Woman's Place*, p. 175.

49. Goode, "Theory of *Role Strain*," p. 486.

50. The legislature meets biennially, and though special sessions are often called in the off year they are generally very short; for example, the 1972 special session met for only 15 days (the regular session in 1971 met for 86 days). The state is very small and the major population centers are all a relatively short commute from the capitol. But beyond these factors it is also apparent that not much is expected of the average member of the assembly.

51. Bailyn, "The Role of Choice," p. 244.

Chapter 5

1. Levinson, "Role, Personality and Social Structure," p. 570.
2. The New York legislature is one of the most professional in the nation. In 1971 the Citizen's Conference on State Legislatures in its comprehensive evaluation of the structures and procedures of state legislatures ranked New York second in the nation (John Burns, *The Sometime Governments* (New York: Bantam Books, 1971), p. 268). In sharp contrast to both Connecticut and New Hampshire, the New York legislature holds full sessions annually. Legislators are paid handsomely ($15,000 annual salary plus $10,000 expense allowance) and are supported by a wide array of staff services. One indication of the desirability of a legislative seat in New York is the low membership turnover. In the 1973 legislative session 31 percent of the assembly members were new, whereas in Connecticut the figure was 40 percent and in New Hampshire 43 percent (the national average was 38 percent). Turnover rates are from *The Book of the States 1974–1975* (Lexington, Ky.: Council of State Governments) p. 69.
3. J. P. McKee and A. C. Sheriffs, "Men's and Women's Beliefs, Ideals, and Self-Concepts," *American Sociologist* 64, no. 4 (1958–59), and J. P. McKee and A. C. Sheriffs, "The Differential Evaluation of Males and Females," *Journal of Personality* 25 (1956–57), as cited in Holter, *Sex Roles*, p. 94; Goldberg's work on the tendency of females to evaluate female achievements less favorably is often cited as an indicator of women's feelings of inferiority (see, for example, Philip Goldberg, "Are Women Prejudiced Against Women?" *Transaction*, April 1968); Lenore J. Weitzman ("Sex-Role Socialization," in Jo Freeman, ed., *Woman: A Feminist Perspective* [Palo Alto: Mayfield Publishing Company, 1975], p. 113), in a discussion of the development of sex-role preferences among children, cites a variety of evidence showing that with increasing age children learn to attach greater prestige and value to the masculine role.
4. Holter, *Sex Roles*, p. 94.
5. Barber, *The Lawmakers*, p. 27. Thirty percent of the spectators were housewives.
6. Ibid., p. 66.
7. Ibid., p. 26.
8. Schlesinger (*Ambition and Politics*, p. 10) develops the concept of progressive political ambitions.
9. Gordon S. Black, "A Theory of Political Ambition: Career Choices and the Role of Structural Incentives" (*American Political Science*

Review 66 [March 1972]), discusses the relationship between net investments and commitment to politics.

10. Barber, *The Lawmakers*, p. 64.

11. Frieda Gehlen ("Man's World," *Transaction* 7 [October 1969], p. 40) found that female congressmen enjoyed casework much more than male congressmen.

12. It is interesting to note that the one housewife-benchwarmer with a college degree was more favorably disposed toward the women's movement than the other housewife-benchwarmers. According to the 1972 Harris Poll, 46 percent of women with a college degree sympathize with the efforts of women's liberation groups, while this is true of 36 percent of women with a high school degree. Harris, *Virginia Slims Opinion Poll*, p. 4.

13. Given her view of women's role in society, it is highly unlikely that the Traditional Civic Worker will run for the legislature when her children are young. Unusual circumstances may allow this; one Traditional Civic Worker in New Hampshire had a young baby, but she lived five blocks from the state house and was married to a prominent physician.

14. Schlesinger, *Ambition and Politics*, p. 175.

15. Barber, *The Lawmakers*, p. 164.

16. Ibid., pp. 80, 81.

17. See "The Two Major Types of Suffragist Argument," in Aileen S. Kraditor, *The Ideas of the Woman Suffrage Movement: 1890–1920* (Garden City, N.Y.: Doubleday, 1971), pp. 38–57.

18. Bailyn, "The Role of Choice," p. 238.

19. I do not have complete data on the political ambitions of advocates because the transcripts from New York did not contain information on ambition for all the legislators.

20. Holter (*Sex Roles*, p. 39) notes: "It may be, however, that one of the reasons why feminism in some ways has failed to change sex differentiation radically, is precisely because the degree of self-righteousness necessary to carry the movement further is too alien to the feminine personality."

21. Barber, *The Lawmakers*, p. 224.

22. "Role Differentiation in Small Groups," in Talcott Parsons and Robert F. Bales, *Family, Socialization, and Interaction Process* (Glencoe, Ill.: Free Press, 1955); "Achieving Group Goals," in Newcomb et al., *Social Psychology*.

23. Parsons and Bales, *Family, Socialization and Interaction Process*, p. 317.

24. Barber, *Lawmakers*, p. 66.

25. Newcomb et al., *Social Psychology*, p. 473.

26. Epstein, *Woman's Place*, p. 195.

27. Hanna Pitkin, *The Concept of Representation* (Berkeley and Los Angeles: University of California Press, 1967), pp. 60–61.
28. Ibid., pp. 113–14.
29. Paul Peterson, "Forms of Representation: Participation of the Poor in the Community Action Program," *American Political Science Review* 64 (June 1970), p. 492.
30. William E. Connolly ("On Interests in Politics," *Politics and Society*, vol. 2, no. 4 [Summer 1972], p. 472) suggests defining the concept of real interests in this manner.
31. As quoted in "New Hampshire Women Legislators 1921–1971," published by the New Hampshire Savings Bank on the golden anniversary of women legislators in New Hampshire, 1971.
32. John Herbers ("First Primary State is Typical and Untypical," *New York Times*, February 22, 1976, sec. 4, p. 1), in discussing the upcoming primary in New Hampshire, notes: "The State government is considered by many to be antediluvian in both organization and policy. It is the only state in the nation with neither a sales or income tax. Half its revenues come from taxes on liquor, cigarettes, dog racing and lotteries. As a result the state ranks 50th in per capita spending on education and has substandard services in several areas."

Chapter 6

1. Kay Boals, "Review Essay Political Science," *Signs* 1 (Autumn 1975), pp. 161–74; Susan Bourque and Jean Grossholtz, "Politics as an Unnatural Practice: Political Science," *Politics and Society* 4 (Winter 1974), pp. 225–66; Jane Jaquette, "Introduction," in Jane Jaquette, ed., *Women in Politics*, (New York: John Wiley, 1974) xiii–xxxvii; Thelma McCormack, "Toward a Nonsexist Perspective on Social and Political Change," in Marcia Millman and Rosabeth Moss Kanter, eds., *Another Voice* (New York: Anchor Books, 1975), pp. 1–33.
2. I would like to suggest for future studies that might test the revised curvilinearity hypothesis that an additional explanation of the relationship between sex differences and competition be considered. The relationship between candidates and party officials is surely dependent on the competitiveness of districts. Party leaders may be in the position to exact conformity to certain performance expectations when the candidate needs the party's support. Since party leaders hold certain attitudes about appropriate styles for women in politics (we know this from the female legislators' reports of interactions with party officials and their legislative colleagues), we might expect female conformity to vary with need of

party support. In the low competition situation the party only cares that a candidate be a warm body and thus the candidate has no incentive to conform. At very high levels of competition the party cannot hand the seat to the candidate or take the seat away, and so again there is no incentive for meeting performance expectations. In contrast, the moderate competition situation may be precisely the one in which conformity is most easily exacted. Party support may be very valuable here, thus making the risks of nonconformity higher. If performance expectations differ for men and women, the differences would be strongest where expectations are most important and therefore most enforceable. I would like to thank Myra Marx Ferree for suggesting this line of inquiry.

3. Delyte Frost ("White Women Only," *DO IT NOW* 9 [April 1976], p. 11) notes the relationship between sex and race: "The racism of white women supports sexism. By working to combat sexism and not working at the same time to combat racism, white women will create a new place in our society for white *only*. This white women's place will continue to be more valued by the white male system than the place of third world women, who will retain the place of third world men. This ultimate racist outcome will also sustain sexism—because by working for that new place for white women and not actively combating white racism, we as white women are saying that we value our whiteness *above our femaleness*" (emphasis in the original).

4. The conflicts taking place within the largest and most developed feminist organization today, the National Organization for Women, may so weaken organized feminism that the question of which scenario will prevail will be moot. Because the situation is in flux it is very difficult to assess what is really occurring, but it appears that the conflict itself may relate to the two scenarios. The faction which gained control of the organization at the 1975 national convention was elected on the platform of "out of the mainstream, into the revolution." Rhetorically this platform certainly differs from the 1966 statement of purpose ("The purpose of NOW is to take action to bring women into full participation in the mainstream of American society now.") The losing faction at the convention felt that the organization could not move too far ahead of the majority of American women and has subsequently formed a "network" call "Womensurge." NOW as an organization has heretofore appeared to defy the social science dictum that social movements become more conservative and routinized as they grow older.

5. Charlotte Bunch ("The Reform Tool Kit," *Quest* 1 [Summer 1974], pp. 40–41) notes: "Fears of co-optation are justified, but sometimes they have resulted in the attempt by many to remain pure, to

be uncorrupted by association with *any* reforms. . . . As a result, we often neglect the creation of conditions that could make these actions more progressive, as well as keep us honest. Purism taken to its extreme results in immobilism and cynicism" (emphasis in the original).

6. For example, the Center for the American Woman and Politics, a part of the Eagleton Institute of Politics at Rutgers University, is a nonpartisan educational and research center established in 1971 to encourage political participation by women; the National Women's Education Fund was formed in 1972 to develop educational and training programs as an aid for women who want to enter public life; the National Women's Political Caucus is a multipartisan membership organization established in 1971 to increase female political participation; state Caucus affiliates now exist in each of the fifty states. The Women's Campaign Fund was established in 1974 to raise money for qualified, progressive women candidates of both major political parties who are candidates for office; the Washington Institute for Women in Politics, Mount Vernon College, was founded in 1975.

I am afraid that my prognosis about parity was borne out all too well by the November 1976 elections. The total percentage of women in state legislatures increased from 8.1 percent to only 9.1 percent.

7. I think that my argument about costs and the size of the pool of candidates is supported by some information on the characteristics of women who were candidates for state and national office in the 1974 primaries. Among the women in the age category 25–35 years, 49 percent had no children. Reported in my paper "Female Candidates in the 1974 Primaries," presented at the Adelphi University Symposium on Women in Politics, September 1975. Marilyn Johnson and Kathy Stanwick (*Profile of Women Holding Office*, New Brunswick. N.J.: Center for the American Woman and Politics, 1976) also observe that among women state legislators in 1975, younger women were *more* likely to be childless than their age cohort in the general population. This development bears watching because heretofore marital patterns of female legislators have not differed from those typical of American women (see Jeane J. Kirkpatrick, *Political Women* (New York: Basic Books, 1974), p. 219).

8. About a week after I wrote these conclusions I discovered that Michelle Zimbalist Rosaldo had come to similar conclusions after her anthropological overview of the status of women in various societies. "If the public world is to open its doors to more than the elite among women, the nature of work itself will have to be al-

tered, and the asymmetry between work and the home reduced" (p. 42). She notes earlier in the same article that "perhaps the most egalitarian societies are those in which public and domestic spheres are only weakly differentiated, where neither sex claims much authority and the focus of social life itself is the home" (p. 36). "Woman, Culture, and Society: A Theoretical Overview," in Michelle Zimbalist Rosaldo and Louise Lamphere, eds., *Woman, Culture and Society* (Stanford: Stanford University Press, 1974).

Index

Abortion, attitudes toward, 50
Achievement: and women's self-images, 118
Advantages of female legislator, 170; in campaigns, 80–83; with colleagues, 98–105
Age: of male and female legislators in New England, 38; of interviewees, 68, 69; effect on women's political careers, 110–11, 131–32, 144; of female legislators, 177. See also Connecticut; New Hampshire
Aggression: in boys, 34; not expected of women, 104; of Women's Rights Advocate, 142
Agriculture committee, assignment of women to, 45
Androgyny, 66, 166
Angrist, Shirley, 62
Anti-politics attitudes in women, 105
Arizona, female legislators in, 20–22
Assertive behavior: sexes compared, 46, 47

Baer, Michael A., 105
Baker v. Carr, 18
Banton, Michael, 66
Barber, James David, 31, 32, 44, 63, 102, 119, 132, 150
Bargaining, attitude toward: sex differences in, 47, 56, 58; and involvement in political parties, 56, 57; not affected by method of recruitment, 58; of Housewife-Benchwarmer, 126; of Traditional Civic Worker, 134, 135; of female lawyers, 168; and interest in women's rights, 169
Beauvoir, Simone de, 66
Blair, Emily Newell: advice to women, 30

Buchanan, William, 63
Bullock, Charles S., 7
Bunch, Charlotte, 206 n 5

Campaigns, 79–84; work in, 42; women's advantages in, 79, 80, 82–84, 85; women's disadvantages in, 81, 84; money in, 84; attitude of Housewife-Benchwarmer toward, 122
Candidates, effect of competition on types of, 60, 61
Catholicism: and abortion, 50, 51
Center for the American Woman and Politics, 207 n 6
Children: of male and female legislators in New England, 38; of interviewees, 68–69; effect on political career, 111, 112; of female legislators, 178; of New England women, 178; of female candidates, 207 n 7
Class: influence of working class in Rhode Island, 19; and political parties, 19, 59; and political participation, 40; differences between Housewife-Benchwarmer and Traditional Civic Worker, 128; women as a, 147, 148, 162; differences possibly intensified in future, 174
Colleagues, female legislator's interactions with, 89–105
Colorado, female legislators in, 29
Commitment to legislative career: sexes compared, 43, 44
Commitment to politics: of Housewife-Benchwarmer, 121, 122; of Traditional Civic Worker, 130–32; of Women's Rights Advocate, 143, 144

209